THE BINARY BRAIN

THE BINARY BRAIN

Artificial Intelligence in the Age of Electronics

DAVID RITCHIE

Little, Brown and Company   Boston—Toronto

FIRST EDITION

Library of Congress Cataloging in Publication Data

Ritchie, David, 1952 Sept. 18-
  The binary brain.

  Bibliography: p.
  Includes index.
  1. Artificial intelligence.   2. Computers.
I. Title.
Q335.R58   1984   001.53'5   83-22194
ISBN 0-316-74730-0

MV

Designed by Patricia Girvin Dunbar

Published simultaneously in Canada
by Little, Brown & Company (Canada) Limited

PRINTED IN THE UNITED STATES OF AMERICA

For Suzanna and Christopher

Contents

Author's Preface

This book grew out of a suggestion from Barry Lippman of Little, Brown, in the autumn of 1981. He wanted to see a book explore the idea that computers are the next step in human evolution — a leap forward equivalent to the development of the cerebral cortex. For that idea I am indebted to him, because it formed a splendid unifying theme for this narrative.

When one is dealing with two branches of human knowledge as arcane and complicated as evolutionary biology and computer science, there is always a risk of distortion through oversimplification. In places this may have occurred, because much of the material discussed here had to be condensed and simplified in the interest of the reader, who probably has no interest in the chemistry of acetylcholine in the nervous system, or algorithms for implementing computational theories.

For that reason, I have included an extensive bibliography and list of suggested readings, in case any readers should wish to pursue the topics discussed here in greater detail than this book allows.

San Leandro, California
August 16, 1982

Acknowledgments

So many persons have helped with the making of this book that it would be impossible to list all of them here. Chief among them are Barry Lippman of Little, Brown; my literary agent, Barbara Bova; and all the specialists in computer science and artificial intelligence who provided fact and opinion while the book was being researched.

THE BINARY BRAIN

The Monster's Riddle | 1

A young man of noble birth was traveling through Greece several centuries before the birth of Christ, and his journey was becoming a nightmare.

He had just received word, from an unimpeachable source, that a terrible fate awaited him at home. So he was running away from everyone and everything he held dear, in order to escape the dreadful doom that had been prophesied for him.

Under those circumstances, the last thing he needed was to come face-to-face with a man-eating monster, and be forced into a battle of wits with the creature at the risk of his own life.

Yet that is precisely what happened to the young traveler. His name was Oedipus. How he came to meet the monster and vanquish it in an intellectual tussle is among the most famous stories in Western literature.

Oedipus was no stranger to bad luck. In fact, his life had started very inauspiciously.

His father was King Laius of Thebes, the Greek city known today as Thívai. Laius's wife Queen Jocasta was Oedipus's mother. When she gave birth to Oedipus, one might have expected Laius to be pleased and to act the role of proud father. But rather than handing out the then equivalent of cigars, Laius reacted fearfully to the news of his son's arrival.

Laius had been warned by an oracle — a soothsayer — that his son would murder him someday. So Laius made up his mind to dispose of the infant before Oedipus could grow up and have a chance to commit regicide.

The king took the boy to a nearby mountain and left him there to die of exposure or to be devoured (Laius hoped) by wild animals. To make sure that the baby could not escape, Laius took the precaution of pinning together Oedipus's ankles with a nail. Apparently this cruel act left Oedipus maimed for life, because his name translates as "swollen foot."

Things looked bleak at that moment for the newborn heir to the throne of Thebes. But fortunately for Oedipus, a passing shepherd noticed him lying in the wilderness and rescued him.

A few years of good fortune followed for Oedipus. He was adopted by King Polybus of nearby Corinth, and was raised as the monarch's son. As far as young Oedipus knew, Polybus was his natural father. The boy was ignorant of the identities of his real parents, and for his ignorance he would one day pay dearly.

Corinth had a temple located conveniently nearby at Delphi, roughly six miles away. A person could start out in the morning from Corinth, have a few words with the oracle, and return home before sundown with no trouble.

One day Oedipus visited Delphi and asked the oracle for a forecast of his future. This was a serious moment for Oedipus, because the Delphic temple was one of the most important in the land, and this oracle was one of the most prestigious of all, for she communicated with the mighty god Apollo.

The oracle was an elderly woman named Pythia. She lived apart from her husband, dressed in fashions rather too young for her, and, unlike many other soothsayers, was distressingly specific in her prophecies. Her words carried almost the weight of a medieval papal bull. Her prophecies could make careers or break them, give new hope to the hopeless, or make the confident despair.

Oedipus despaired when he heard her warning. Speaking ex cathedra, she prophesied that one day Oedipus would murder his father and share a conjugal bed with his mother.

Horrified, Oedipus resolved that he would never return home to

Corinth, for fear of committing both patricide and incest. Instead he headed for Thebes, his birthplace — unaware that in trying to flee from his fate, he was in fact running straight toward it.

In quick succession, the oracle's forecasts came true.

On the road to Thebes, Oedipus met a party of three men. One rode in a carriage, while the other two preceded him on the road for the purpose of shoving approaching travelers out of his way.

Oedipus got shoved. Then, as now, young scions of royal families did not take kindly to being pushed around, and Oedipus took his staff and clouted the man who had pushed him. The man in the carriage then used *his* staff to hit Oedipus.

The fight escalated from there, and in a few moments Oedipus had killed all three of his adversaries. He had no way of knowing that one of the dead, the man in the carriage, was his own natural father, King Laius, and that the first part of the oracle's prophecy had just unfolded.

Battered but undaunted, Oedipus left the corpses behind him and continued on the road to Thebes. But on arriving there, he learned another piece of distressing news. The gods had sent a monster to plague Thebes, and the beast was sitting beside the highway and dining on passersby.

The monster was the Sphinx. As monsters went, she was a patchwork job, assembled from parts of several different species: she had a woman's head, a lion's body, and according to some reports, an eagle's wings as well. Daughter of the snake-woman Echidna and her son Orthus, the Sphinx went through a strange ritual with every traveler who was luckless enough to meet her.

The Sphinx asked her potential meals a riddle: "What walks on four legs in the morning, two legs at noon, and three legs in the evening?" Anyone who was unable to think of the correct answer became food for the monster.

Thus far, that meant everyone. Until Oedipus appeared, every last person the Sphinx interrogated had drawn a blank and been devoured. This is not surprising, since it is hard to think cleverly when a terrifying creature is sitting a few feet away from you, licking her chops.

Oedipus, however, kept his wits about him. Having just had a dismal fate foretold for him at Delphi, and having come within an inch of being killed on the road, he was probably ready for anything else that might beset him, the Sphinx included.

The Sphinx anticipated that Oedipus would be merely one more luncheon. So she put the riddle to him, then waited in sweet contemplation while Oedipus thought it over.

For a long moment there was no noise, except the rustle of leaves in the wind, and the songs of birds in nearby trees. Then something clicked in the mind of Oedipus. Turning to the Sphinx and looking her straight in the eye, he said one word:

"Man."

That was, of course, the answer to the Sphinx's riddle. In the morning of life a human baby crawls on all fours. At life's noontide, adulthood, a person walks on two legs. And in old age, when faltering steps mandate the use of a cane, a man walks on three legs, one of them artificial.

Her conundrum solved at last, the Sphinx — apparently unable to think of any other riddles — turned her teeth and claws on herself and committed suicide. Thebes was free of the awful beast and, in gratitude, made Oedipus king.

His bride was the newly widowed Queen Jocasta, his natural mother, whose husband — King Laius — Oedipus had killed on the highway earlier that day. Thus the second part of the oracle's warning came true: Oedipus became his mother's husband. Years later, after Oedipus and Jocasta had had four children together, the truth of their relationship was revealed. Jocasta chose suicide, while Oedipus blinded himself and left Thebes.

Was there really a King Oedipus? Or was his story merely a myth? Whether or not he actually lived, his legend is still interesting for what it tells us about the classical concept of intelligence — particularly human intelligence.

In the tale of Oedipus and the Sphinx we see the human intellect, that vast collection of mental skills, which we also know as "intelligence" or "the mind," as the all-important factor that sets us above other animals, represented here by the Sphinx.

Oedipus defeated the Sphinx, not by strength, nor by speed, nor by agility, but by acumen. Sheer brainpower gives him the crucial edge over the monster. And with one well-chosen word he drives the Sphinx — which has formidable fangs and claws but is so stupid that she can ask only one question — to self-destruction.

Since even before Oedipus's day, scholars have celebrated human intelligence as something wonderfully unique in the animal kingdom: a divine or semidivine spark denied to other creatures and reserved for our species alone. The psalmist remarked that man's intelligence had "given him dominion over the earth, and placed all things under his feet."

In the first century A.D., philosopher Marcus Manilius exulted in the powers of the intelligence: "No barriers, no masses of matter however enormous, can withstand the powers of the mind; the remotest corners yield to them; the very heaven itself is laid open." More than fifteen hundred years later, John Milton, speaking through the character of Satan in *Paradise Lost,* hailed the transforming powers of the human intellect:

> The mind is its own place, and in itself
> Can make a heav'n of hell, a hell of heav'n.

Lovely words, indeed. But if one is going to praise something, one ought to know at least what that something is. And here we must confront the great mystery of intelligence: what *is* it?

Intelligence is one of the most important concepts we know. Everyone respects it in individuals; everyone would like to have as much of it as possible. And everyone seems to know, in a very general way, what intelligence, or intelligent behavior, is. But defining it can be almost as hard a task as trying to nail smoke to the floor.

Yet the more difficult the job, the greater its challenge and allure. And so philosophers have tried for centuries to conquer that intellectual Everest, the nature of the intellect, and figure out just what intelligence really is.

Henri Bergson called intelligence "man's main characteristic" and defined it roughly as the ability to make artificial tools. But what separates a "natural" from an "artificial" tool? Certainly a chain saw or power drill is an artificial tool, while a beak or claw is a natural one. But what about the twig that a chimpanzee breaks off from a tree and uses to pry insects out of a stump or the earth? The twig is not the same twig that it was while still attached to the tree. The chimpanzee broke off the twig and, in a sense, made something artificial of it.

Does this mean that the chimpanzee shares our "main characteristic," intelligence? Not everyone would say yes to that proposition.

Anton Chekhov, pondering the nature of intelligence while making his rounds as a physician, settled for a less precise definition of what makes one intelligent — so imprecise, in fact, as to be nearly meaningless. He defined an intelligent person as one who can "think honestly, feel, and work." That definition could be stretched to cover everything from a cockney to a cockroach. A termite munching on a house beam, for example, is working, feeling, and presumably sincere in whatever passes for its thought. Is the termite therefore intelligent? On polishing off a frame home, does the termite proclaim, "A good house, but not a great house"? Chekhov would probably have said no.

Ralph Waldo Emerson described intelligence as freedom. "So far as a man thinks," wrote Emerson, "he is free." Emerson might have thought differently, had he lived to see millions of men and women thrown into prisons and liquidation camps for the "crime" of thinking freely.

Spinoza gave it his best shot, but his definition of intelligence came to little more than a gassy string of generalities. "There is no rational life without intelligence," he said, "and things are good only insofar as they assist man to enjoy that life of the mind that is determined by intelligence."

Scientists have fared no better than philosophers, where pinning down intelligence is concerned. Animal-behavior experts might say that intelligence is "unpredictability." That makes some sense. The more intelligent an animal is, the less predictably it behaves — on an individual basis, anyway. The actions of a moth or grasshopper are much easier to predict than those of a cat or dog, and so we say that the cat or dog is more intelligent than the insect.

But that criterion breaks down quickly when one notes the behavior of some "unintelligent" things. Consider the electrons whirling about the nucleus of an atom. It is all but impossible to say how each individual electron will behave. Likewise, no one can predict the path a given raindrop will follow on its descent from the clouds. The drop's point of impact is highly uncertain, until it hits the ground. Should we conclude, then, that electrons and raindrops have intelligence? Not many of us would care to admit that our "main characteristic" belongs to falling blobs of water, too.

What about "problem-solving ability"? That test of intelligence was popular for a while, and within certain limitations it works. The more advanced the intelligence, the more subtle and complex problems it can solve. No one could seriously imagine a worm or a water beetle calculating the square root of 3 or carrying out a word-association test.

On the other hand, the choice of problem to be solved does much to determine how intelligent a creature seems. Take an American physicist with a tested intelligence quotient (IQ) of 200, and set him down completely naked in the middle of the Australian outback, with nothing but his much-vaunted wits to support him. Would his demonstrated verbal and mathematical aptitude enable him to find water and food — two very important problems — before he dehydrated or starved to death?

Probably not. "Problem-solving ability," then, has its drawbacks as a way of reckoning intelligence. But however one describes intelligence, the fact remains that we owe almost everything to it. If the world really does lie at our feet, as the psalmist said, then it does so largely because of what we have in our heads: a power of conscious thought that seems unmatched in the animal kingdom.

No other species, so far as we know, can juggle so much information quite so adeptly as we can. It is hard to imagine a chipmunk writing a sonnet, or a lemur pondering the unity of space and time. Mental tasks like those are *our* domain entirely, unless great surprises lurk within the skulls of our fellow creatures.

How our species achieved the pinnacle of mental might on earth is a long and engrossing story, full of unexpected twists of plot. And today the story is reaching its most exciting point, because humans are using their technology to boost their thinking capability — and thus move themselves a rung further up on the evolutionary ladder.

In short, a species — for the first time in the history of life — is consciously and deliberately taking the next step in its own evolution.

Already the results of this move have been more impressive than anyone could have imagined a generation ago. Not even the farseeing Delphic oracle could have envisioned what science and engineering are doing now to expand human brainpower.

And the future may hold advances in intellectual capacity that are beyond our most fantastic dreams today. In a very few years we may see the evolution of a "binary brain," a synthesis of human and machine intelligence, with the strengths of both, and with an intellectual potential as far beyond our present level as we are beyond that of a gorilla or chimpanzee.

We appear to stand at a fateful stage in the evolution of the human brain and mind. If we succeed in taking the next step upward, we will very likely face a future of inconceivable wonders, a golden gateway opening out into the cosmos. And if we fail, then the universe will probably write us off as just another unsuccessful experiment.

The Story So Far | 2

"Begin at the beginning," advised the King of Hearts in *Alice's Adventures in Wonderland*. The history of intelligence has no distinct opening, but a good place to start is in Pacific Canada, near the U.S. border in British Columbia. Here, underneath the green hills and low gray clouds, some of the first stages in the evolution of intelligence can be found in the rocks beside the roads.

The evidence is easy to find. It lies in the famous Burgess shale, a paleontologist's paradise, where a happy accident of geology preserved priceless traces of sea life from the Paleozoic, the first age of life on earth, almost as clearly as if the creatures were still alive.

Drive east from Vancouver, and in a few hours you will arrive at a set of undistinguished-looking outcrops alongside the highway: undistinguished, that is, except for the scattering of fossil hunters clambering over it, hammers in hand. These rocks are to students of ancient fauna what Hollywood is to aspiring actors and actresses. Heaven, to paleontologists, is a mansion on top of the Burgess shale.

Brown and gray shales, fine-grained rocks with a slightly musty smell about them, slant up and down at gentle angles, tilted by the same forces that pushed up the hills and mountains along British Columbia's coast. The rocks barely feel like rock at all. They are soft and crumbly and can be reduced to powder between one's fingers. The shale can be split neatly along its bedding plane — the direction

11

parallel to what was the sea floor when the sediments were laid down millions of years ago.

Part the rock carefully, and in it you may see a dark stain that was once an animal. On dying, the creature fell to the ocean bottom and was covered with fine sediment before its body could decay. The soft body, of course, was crushed, but its image remained in the silt and clay as a carbon imprint, slightly distorted, of the animal's form.

Some of the species entombed here look bizarre to modern eyes. Here is the stain of a jellyfish, which, in life, looked exactly like a floating pineapple ring. Nearby lie the ghostly remains of a trumpet-shaped siphon feeder, which in life stood on the sea floor with its "bell" pointed straight up, sucking in drifting bits of organic material. Some of the beings outlined here look vaguely familiar — distant relatives of our present-day snails and clams and corals. But others resemble nothing now in the seas — like that unidentified thing, about plum-sized, which comes close in appearance to a hot dog with a spherical bun.

Perhaps the weirdest exhibit in this extinct zoo is the fossil of an animal roughly the size of a modern caterpillar. At first glance it looks like a worm. Then one notices the double row of long spines running along its underside. The spines served as legs, so that the animal walked on stilts, so to speak, across the bottom. Along its back stood a row of tentacles, and at the end of each tentacle was a mouth. How the animal ate with this arrangement, it is hard to say. The whole organism looks so unlikely that scientists call it *Hallucinogaea*.

Outlandish as it looks, *Hallucinogaea* tells us much about the way our own intelligence evolved.

Look at the layout of the animal. Running along the length of its body was a nerve cord. Presumably that nerve cord acted just as nerve cords do in wormlike marine animals today, taking in data in the form of nerve impulses from sensory cells along the body, and sending out motor impulses to muscles.

Also, if the fossil in the Canadian rocks is any indication, *Hallucinogaea* had a head, and in it, something like a brain. Brains and heads are all but inseparable in animal architecture, for a very good reason. In that position, the brain is close to the clusters of sensory cells at the forward end of the body, and so short stretches of nerves suffice to link those cells to the brain. (The nervous systems of all animals follow this same principle: never use a long nerve when a short nerve will do.)

Hallucinogaea's brain was unimpressive by human standards. Most likely it consisted of merely a slight swelling of the front end of the nerve cord, like the terminal knob on a walking stick. The brain of this animal probably contained no more than a few thousand cells. It allowed the organism to scent food and to walk about on the bottom mud, but not much more than that.

Nonetheless, we see in this odd little fossil the beginnings of a pattern that would lead ultimately to the human brain and mind.

A nerve cord extending the length of the body, with an enlargement at the anterior end to handle certain specialized functions: that is how our own central nervous system is laid out. So are those of most other animals as well. As a general rule, the size and complexity of the forward swelling corresponds to the degree of intelligence.

Hallucinogaea shared the Paleozoic seas with many other forms of life. Some of them were similar to modern aquatic species such as fishes and lobsters. In these organisms the brain was well developed compared to those of the lowly wormlike crawlers preserved in the Burgess shale. And as the Paleozoic progressed, a trend emerged in the evolution of brains: the brain tended to grow steadily in both size and capability.

Naturally, this trend is no surprise. It is the virtually inevitable outcome of the process of evolution by natural selection — commonly known as "survival of the fittest." We will explore evolution in greater detail later, but for now it suffices to say that a bigger and more sophisticated brain makes a species "fitter" by giving the animal a wider repertory of behavior patterns — a bigger bag of tricks, so to speak — and consequently a better chance of survival. Because the big brain enhances survival, it will be passed along to the animal's offspring and thus will be perpetuated in generations to come.

Quick wits were required in the Paleozoic seas, for the ocean, then as now, was full of hungry hunters, and life there was a fierce and endless fight for food. A species had to look ceaselessly for food, and at the same time, try to avoid becoming food for other animals.*

The biological environment, then, was thoroughly hostile in this first age of life. And as the Paleozoic neared its end, roughly 250 million years ago, danger approached from another side as well. Now the physical environment also posed a threat to survival — and this grim development turned out to have stupendous implications for the evolution of brains and higher intelligence.

The cause is still unclear, but the fossil record suggests that the once hospitable seas dried up over much of the world's area. Possibly the continents were rearranging themselves and squeezing seas out of existence in the process. Whatever the reason, sea life suddenly faced a problem: how to survive in a desiccating world?

The answer was, learn to live with it. This the aquatic animals of the late Paleozoic did. They developed lungs to enable themselves to function in the air, and legs to carry themselves across stretches of dry land between wet, hospitable surroundings of seas and lakes and rivers.

To handle the switch from aquatic to terrestrial environments, marine creatures became amphibians. The change was demanding. Not only did the amphibians have to hold on to all the brain functions required for life in the sea, but they had to tackle the challenge of temporary life on land as well. As fins turned into legs, new motor skills were needed, for walking on the beach is quite a different proposition from paddling along through the water. New sensory powers were needed as well; for in the milieu of the land, where the big enemy was not a clawed, toothed predator, but rather the blind, inanimate factors of heat and cold and aridity, the race for survival would inevita-

---

* Sometimes the need for vigilance led to bizarre adaptations. Many good examples are found among the trilobites, hard-shelled Paleozoic creatures roughly equivalent to present-day crabs and crayfish. One species of trilobite evolved a single mammoth compound eye (made up of many individual lenses, like those of some insects), which was wrapped around the front of the head and gave the trilobite a field of vision exceeding 300 degrees! Humans, by contrast, can see through only about a 200-degree arc.

bly be won by the amphibians who were best attuned to their physical environment. Nature would award survival to those who could best recognize danger (say, the sudden change in humidity that means a dry wind is coming, and it's time to return to the pond) and opportunity, such as the approach of another animal that might provide a meal.

So the amphibians were forced to develop bigger and more capable brains than their purely aquatic ancestors had. Amphibians needed greater intelligence, for they had to make the best of *two* worlds, land and water.

Look at the contrast in brain size between fishes and amphibians today. A trout has a brain about the size of a green pea. It weighs approximately one gram, or as much as a paper clip.

In the frog, the brain has swelled two- to fivefold, to more than the weight of a penny. Slight as this difference may seem to humans, it shows what a great step forward the amphibians had taken on the scale of brain evolution. And even greater advances were just ahead.

The amphibians were only a transitional form between life in the water and life on land. To take full advantage of conditions on the dry earth, animals would have to leave the seas entirely, and learn to compete full-time in the terrestrial realm. And to do so they would need still bigger and more versatile brains to cope with the rigors of that new environment.

The result: reptiles.

Reptiles colonized the land so successfully that the Mesozoic, the "middle age" of life in between the Paleozoic and our own Cenozoic "age of mammals," is often called the "age of reptiles." The Mesozoic was the time of the dinosaurs — the tyrannosaurs, brontosaurs, pterodactyls, and all the other favorites of Saturday afternoon TV viewers.

Whether the dinosaurs were really reptiles or not is a question that bedevils paleontologists. Though some dinosaur species do resemble lizards, right down to the fine internal structure of their bones, many others — including some small, fleet flesh-eaters similar in form to the roadrunners of the American Southwest — were so clearly adapted to life at high speed that it is hard to see how they could have functioned as reptiles, which tend to have sluggish metabolisms. So perhaps it is misleading to lump dinosaurs all together into the category of reptiles.

It is equally mistaken to say that all dinosaurs were stupid. Undoubtedly some of them were, even by saurian standards. The tank-sized *Stegosaurus,* a plant-eater adorned with large bony plates along its spine and a small arsenal of spikes on its tail, had a brain no larger than a walnut. Indeed, its cranial capacity was so small that the dinosaur required a second "brain" at the base of its legs to handle the motions of its massive hindquarters.

Most of the dinosaurs familiar to the general public fall into the big-and-stupid category: *Diplodocus,* with its monumental body and tiny lump of a head, *Tyrannosaurus,* all teeth and no brain; and so forth. Some scientists doubt these monsters were even conscious. Conceivably, they just lumbered around in something approaching a sleepwalking state, what brains they had operating, one might say, on automatic pilot.

Less well known, but more interesting from our point of view, are some brainier members of the dinosaur clan. These species, given a few million more years, might have evolved an intelligence comparable to our own. A good example is *Stenonychosaurus,* a meat-eating dinosaur that appeared in the late Mesozoic, just before the early mammals, our remote ancestors, took over the world. A *Stenonychosaurus* skeleton is eerie to see. Picture something like a modern ostrich, but with an elongated reptilian tail stretching out behind. In front are two hands: perhaps not quite hands like ours, but very similar appendages with long, agile fingers capable of grasping small, ratlike animals and lifting such prey to the dinosaur's mouth. Looking at the hands of *Stenonychosaurus,* one can almost imagine it playing a harp in dinosaur heaven.

The most striking thing about this dinosaur, however, is its skull. It is a big skull, as those of dinosaurs go: the brain it housed accounted for about a thousandth part of the animal's body weight. Some of the larger plant-eaters, at the opposite end of the brain-body scale, were only about 1/200,000 brain by weight. (A human being built on the same proportions would have a brain weighing about 0.014 ounces, or about as much as a bit of dandelion fluff.)

The big brain of *Stenonychosaurus* was vital to its way of life, for this dinosaur was a fast-moving predator, probably hunting at night when its food, small nocturnal mammals, became most active. The dinosaur had to spot its quarry in the darkness, make an accurate estimate of distance and the speed required to make a successful catch, and then grab the little animal with lightning swiftness.

For this demanding set of tasks, the dinosaur needed a complicated brain. Just how complicated, we can gather from the fact that this dinosaur had stereo vision. Its eyes were set in the front of its head, as ours are, and had overlapping fields of vision so that the dinosaur could spot a running meal from two slightly different angles at once. The brain compared the two images, measured the discrepancy between them, and used it to figure the distance to the target.

This is not the work of a feeble spoonful of nerve tissue like the brontosaur's brain. *Stenonychosaurus* had a good brain and used it. So, for that matter, did several other known species of dinosaurs built along the same lines as *Stenonychosaurus*. It seems that toward the end of the Mesozoic, a fair number of big-brained dinosaur species were roaming the globe.

Look at their skulls, face-on, and you will feel a faint chill, as Hamlet did looking at Yorick. The big eye sockets and oversized craniums give these saurian skulls all too close a resemblance to our own. Perhaps behind those oversized eyes lurked something like a mind.

What the descendants of *Stenonychosaurus* and its kin might have looked like, we can only guess. Dinosaurs like this one were well on the way to developing an intelligence comparable to ours when something cut short their progress. The dinosaurs became extinct.

The death of the dinosaurs is one of the greatest mysteries of geology. Scientists have proposed dozens of theories, of which climate change seems the most likely possibility.

Apparently the dinosaurs lived in a world much warmer than ours. Mean global temperature during the Mesozoic probably stood a few degrees higher than it does today. Therefore the dinosaurs, accustomed to a warm climate, would have found themselves at a disadvantage if the climate cooled sharply; and if the fossil record is any indication, the earth *did* cool off dramatically as the Mesozoic neared its end.

Here and there in the Mesozoic strata, one can see signs of a global cold snap just before the dinosaurs disappeared. Sometimes the transition between Mesozoic and Cenozoic is as sharp as a knife cut: warm-weather flora and fauna give way to other organisms adapted to life in chillier climes, within the space of a few millimeters of rock. The contrast is like finding beach sandals next to snowshoes in a closet.

When the age of dinosaurs ended, our age of mammals began. Suddenly the mammals, warm-blooded animals with furry coats and the practice of suckling their young, found themselves in possession of a world.

Heretofore the dinosaurs, as unchallenged masters of land and sea and sky, had shut out the mammals from all the choicest ecological niches, in much the same way that a giant corporation fears no competition from the corner garage or newsstand. The mammals had been forced to make do in the tiny nooks and crannies, one might say, of the dinosaurs' world. But with the dinosaurs gone, the early mammals finally had the opportunity to spread out, diversify, and fill the ecological roles left vacant by the dinosaurs' departure.

These original mammals did not look promising. The few fossils (mostly teeth and jawbones) that have survived from the early Cenozoic indicate the first mammals were little and ratlike, ranging in size from that of a shrew up to perhaps a muskrat. When you see a common rat skitter along a country road, you are looking back some sixty million years.

But the mammals quickly took advantage of their unexpected good luck, and very soon they were following the very same course of evolution the reptiles had taken some 200 million years earlier. The mammals changed their forms to colonize virtually every environment on the planet, from the blistering deserts to the polar seas. And as they diversified, they were building up their brains.

Brains they needed, probably more than the dinosaurs did, for the Cenozoic was a tougher time. Gone was the warm and generally benevolent climate that had typified the Mesozoic, replaced with a much harsher regime.

From time to time, ice ages plunged the world into millennia-long winters of endless ice and snow. Even during warm spells between ice ages, the mercury fell short of Mesozoic levels, and this cooler world was far more tempestuous than the age of dinosaurs had been.

When tyrannosaurs roamed the earth and pteranodons cruised the skies, there was no sharp temperature gradient between the equator and the poles. The lower latitudes were hot, and the upper latitudes were warm. As a result, much of the world was one big Bermuda. If anyone ever arranges for trips by time machine, the Mesozoic will probably make a popular vacation spot, balmy and relatively free from storms.

The Cenozoic cooling, however, changed this idyllic situation. What climatologists call the "latitudinal temperature gradient" rose sharply. That is, the poles were now colder relative to the equator than they had been during the Mesozoic. In a manner of speaking, the upper latitudes were hungrier for heat, and more heat had to be transported poleward from the tropics to keep the earth's energy budget balanced. As all that warmth rushed toward the ends of the earth, swept along by winds and ocean currents, warmth and water vapor combined to stir up storms between the hot tropics and cold poles. The result was a more violent, hostile, and unpredictable climate — which in turn had an important effect on the minds of the dinosaurs' heirs.

A brontosaur had the assurance that each day's weather would probably be much like the day before. But the Cenozoic mammals had no such guarantee. Theirs was a more risky environment, and they had to be ready for anything it might dish out, from hurricanes to hailstorms, deluges to droughts. And consequently the mammals needed bigger and better brains to cope with rapidly changing conditions.

Look at the skeletons of mammals and dinosaurs, and you will see how dramatically they differ in brain size. As a rule, a typical mammal has several times more brain per pound or kilogram of body than the dinosaurs had. In the brontosaur and its even bigger cousins, one gram of brain controlled perhaps a ton of body. The largest living mammal, the blue whale, has *ninety* grams of brain for each ton of muscle, bone, and blubber: almost two whole orders of magnitude more than the giant dinosaur's brain/body ratio.

Of course, this ratio is much higher in many smaller mammals. The house cat, for example, has about a 1:100 brain/body ratio; a dinosaur with the same ratio might have had a one-ton brain and been unable to lift its heavy head off the ground.

There is a lesson in these figures, and it is basically what the moralists have been saying for centuries. Adversity can be a good thing.

In this case, harsh climate gave mammals an impetus to build up their brains. Exactly how the mammals did it was a mystery until the mid-nineteenth century. And while one man usually gets the credit for first realizing how species evolve intelligence, in fact he was only one of several scientists who solved the puzzle of evolution. Their stories demonstrate that scientists — to put it charitably — are just as human as anyone else.

The Big Little Difference | 3

He was short by modern standards, and his skull had a peculiar shape. It bulged outward in back, and in front had room for only the tiniest of foreheads. Huge brow ridges overhung his eyes, which were bright blue and once had shone with delight at the sight of his children playing in the sunlight.

But his eyes were shut now, and the brain inside his odd-shaped skull would never perceive anything again.

A blow from a club had shattered the rear of his cranium, killing him instantly. The murderer was one of the tall strangers who lately had been invading his lands. The newcomers had high foreheads, and their weapons were strange and deadly; their traps and snares killed without warning, and one noticed them only when it was too late to escape.

A few minutes earlier, one of the high-browed men had crouched alongside the path on which the dead man's body now lay. The ambusher knew this was a well-traveled artery, and so he had expected he would spot a victim soon — with luck, one who was carrying food or something else of value. Shrewdly, the club-wielding highwayman concealed himself in the undergrowth, and was careful to place himself downwind from the path, so that the stink of his body would not give away his hiding place.

He had only a short wait. A few minutes after he went into hiding, he saw the slightly stooped figure of one of the low-browed locals, ambling along the path and carrying a fish caught in a nearby pond. An ideal dinner, the robber thought.

It was over in two seconds. A leap, a swift and sure blow to the traveler's head, and the killer had his meal. He looked down at the corpse with no pangs of compassion; after all, these creatures looked so repulsive that killing one was practically a public service.

Fish in one hand, club in the other, the man strode away homeward to his wife and children, to tell them what wonderfully good luck he had had.

This little melodrama is an imagined encounter, but something very much like it took place some thousands of years ago in the Afro-Eurasian land mass, as one branch of the human species gained the upper hand over its competition. You are here today, reading this book, because one side in this conflict happened to have a slight edge in intelligence over the other.

Just over a century ago, a handful of scientists uncovered the secret of how intelligence evolved. The main player in this drama was Charles Darwin, the naturalist who usually is credited with working out the theory of evolution by natural selection — more widely known as "evolution" or as "survival of the fittest."

Basically, this is what Darwin said. Species are constantly changing their forms and capabilities — longer legs here, a broader leaf there. If these changes help the species survive, then the individuals bearing them will have an advantage in the fight for existence, and will pass the helpful traits on to their offspring. If new traits do not favor survival — and very few of them do — then they will be weeded out as the organisms that possess them are killed. The fittest survive. The unfit perish. Period.

Darwin's theory was actually much more complicated and subtle, but this summary conveys the essence of it. Nature is constantly weeding out the variations that reduce the chances of a creature's survival, and awarding success to the very few lucky species and individuals whose variations come in handy.

Looking at humans in light of Darwin's ideas, one might wonder how our species endured at all. A naked human being is a rather un-impressive animal. We have no armor to discourage predators, no natural weapons like the porcupine's quills or the stegosaur's spiked tail, no mighty fangs to aid in catching food. Compared to the dog or cheetah, we are pathetic runners. At night we are practically blind. Our bodies give off such strong odors that tracking us down is no problem for most carnivores. We can barely smell anything our-selves; our olfactory sense is much weaker than that of the dog or cat. Our hearing is poor by the standards of most other creatures. We lack thick hides to protect against wounds, and heavy fur to withstand cold weather.

How, then, did we survive as a species?

Fortunately, while we were underendowed with teeth, hair, and so forth, we evolved an excess of an even more valuable trait: intelli-gence.

It was an intangible trait, but it made up for all the natural survival aids we lacked. We had no need of saber teeth when we could make spears and knives. Those tools, in turn, remedied many of our other natural shortcomings; for example, we could hunt down animals and skin them to provide body covering. We had no use for keen night vision when, by taming fire, we could light the night artificially. And so forth.

In short, mindpower was better protection than the tyrannosaur's teeth ever were. It was the most useful survival aid of them all. Like any other helpful trait, intelligence was passed along from genera-tion to generation, until humans were the undisputed bosses of the planet. And eventually human intelligence, in the persons of Charles Darwin and his colleagues, took on the monumental task of trying to figure out its own origins.

The overall pattern of evolution — intelligence included — was worked out independently by Darwin and a younger natural-ist, Alfred Russel Wallace. Their formulations of the theory of evolu-tion were almost identical and were published jointly. Darwin was by far the more colorful figure of the two men, and the story of his achievements — his globe-girdling voyage on HMS *Beagle,* his exhaustive studies of the animal kingdom, his spiritual crisis at discovering a conflict between church doctrine and the evidence of the natural world — has been told in detail elsewhere. Less widely known are the stories of Darwin's chief lieutenant in the fight over evolutionary theory — Thomas Henry Huxley — and of what Darwin's followers did to the work and reputation of a gifted French biologist who undeservedly became a whipping boy for later scientists.

Huxley, who came to be known as "Darwin's bulldog" for his fervent support of Darwinian theory, was one of Britain's most famous biologists, authors, and educators. The ancestor of Aldous and Julian, Thomas Huxley was seen as a demon by many Victorians and a secular saint by many others, and did as much as Darwin himself to win acceptance for Darwinism. As we will see later, Huxley also foresaw how human intelligence might develop in the future, and even how a human intellect might be copied within a machine — a goal that gave rise to a whole new science after the Second World War.

Huxley is remembered best for his role in winning the debate between Creationists (those who believed a divine Creator conjured up the world and all it contains, just as one sees them today, out of pure nothingness) and the backers of Darwinism. Darwin, in his books *On the Origin of Species* and *The Descent of Man*, contended that the evidence of the biological and physical world contradicted the Creationist point of view; that in fact one found in the animal kingdom an upward progression of development, from small and simple organisms to larger and more complex ones. Humans, Darwin argued, appeared to be no special creation of the Divinity, but rather just the latest in a long line of evolutionary progressions running upward through the primate family. Even that alleged spark of Godhead, the human mind, Darwin saw as nothing more than one more step in evolution. "There is no fundamental difference between man and the higher animals in their mental faculties," wrote Darwin in *The Descent of Man*. Our thinking apparatus isn't much different from that of a monkey or chimpanzee, Darwin said; we just happen to have a little more of it, that's all. W. Winwood Reade, in his book *The Martyrdom of Man*, put it more pointedly: "If we look into ourselves we discover propensities that declare that our intellects have arisen from a lower form. Could our minds be made visible, we should find them tailed."

This hypothesis — humans descended (or ascended, if one prefers) from more primitive primates — enraged some factions of the Church, which saw in Darwinism a threat to established thought in which the clergy had a vested interest. Since before Galileo, the Church had seen its comforting doctrines attacked and demolished one by one, as science took on superstition and decked it. Copernicus and Kepler had shown the Church's geocentric model of the universe, with the earth at its center, to be a fraud, and by the mid-1800s the clergy was still uncomfortable with the idea that the earth might be only one insignificant speck of rock in an endless cosmos. Now Darwin and Huxley threatened to go even farther, and dethrone humankind from its special place in God's creation. Darwinists would admit nothing divine about the human species. And if the Church went along with Darwinism, and admitted humans were merely the pride of the primates, then what would be the use of having a church? Churches owe their existence — that is, their income — to the idea of a special relationship between humans and God; and Darwin, by casting that relationship into doubt, seemed to be shaking the foundations of the whole Christian religion as well. Incensed, the clergy sallied forth to meet Darwin in mortal combat. Unfortunately for them, they met not Darwin, but Huxley.*

Huxley and Darwin were opposites in many respects. Darwin was born wealthy; Huxley was the product of a lower-class family, and had had to fight his way upward to distinction. Darwin looked small, fragile, and kindly, his long white beard giving him the image of a trim Santa Claus. Huxley stood well over six feet tall, wore huge side-whiskers, and was capable of freezing opponents with a single scowl. Huxley was an intimidating presence as well as the model of a sober, respectable Victorian scientist; when he walked into a room, conversation tended to stop as everyone turned to look at the tower-

---

* In time, the Church of England realized that there was no irreconcilable difference between Darwinism and church doctrine, and granted Darwin a church funeral.

ing biologist with the penetrating eyes. In any case, Huxley could put an end to conversation fast, with a few tart words; unlike Darwin, who was not especially quick at repartee, Huxley had a sarcastic wit that could slice through bone.

Most importantly, Huxley loved a scrap, whereas Darwin was a coward who did his best to avoid controversy. A born provocateur, Huxley delighted in baiting clerics in whom he found an anti-scientific attitude. Once he heard that a well-known Creationist bishop had died after falling off a horse and landing on his head. "His Grace's mind has come into contact with reality for the first time," Huxley noted. "As might have been expected, the result was fatal." Huxley dubbed himself *Episcophagus* — "bishop-eater" — and once made an eminently satisfying meal of Samuel Wilberforce, one of the clerical champions of Creationism.

Bishop Wilberforce of Oxford, a man of such personal charm and persuasive rhetoric that he was known as "Soapy Sam," turned his formidable powers of argument on Huxley in a public debate over Darwinism — and might have won the day for Creationism, had anyone but Huxley opposed him.

When Wilberforce had the floor, the audience's feelings seemed overwhelmingly in his favor. Thus encouraged, Wilberforce grew overconfident, and without knowing it, handed Huxley the rope with which to hang him.

Was it, the bishop gibed, "through his grandfather or his grandmother that he [Huxley] claimed his descent from a monkey?"

At that moment Huxley knew victory was his. "The Lord," Huxley mumbled, "hath delivered him into mine hands!"

Huxley then rose and replied that he would rather be descended from a monkey than from "a man who used great gifts to obscure the truth."* Suddenly Wilberforce's sarcasm sounded hollow. The hall erupted in applause for Huxley, who in a few well-chosen words had mown down the Creationists and their leader. Even the clergy had to admit that Huxley had won the day.

---

* Huxley's rejoinder sounds much like the reply Alexandre Dumas Père gave to a rude question about his ancestry: "My father was a Creole, his father was a Negro, and his father was a monkey. It seems, sir, that my family starts where yours left off."

Inspired by Huxley's example, other Darwinists joined the fray, and soon the anti-Darwinists were in full retreat. Darwin himself had backed his theory with so many concrete illustrations from the natural world that his defenders found it easy to smash their opposition in the Creationist camp. Unfortunately, they also smashed the reputation of an earlier biologist whose work foreshadowed Darwin's own.

His name was Jean Baptiste de Lamarck. He died in 1829 in Paris, penniless and largely forgotten by his peers. In his lifetime he was known as a masterful botanist. His portraits show an unremarkable face framed by a nondescript wig; his expression is impatient, and understandably so, for Lamarck was a person of action, and it probably annoyed him to be immobilized for a portrait session.

Lamarck had a great idea, and an error in interpretation did much to deprive him of credit for it. He also fell victim to a malicious campaign of half-truths and distortions, waged by a hostile camp of scientists years after his death. And without realizing it, he helped to create a model of evolution that applies not to the biological world, but rather to a world of inventions he could never have foreseen.

Lamarck was born into a middle-class French family during the tumultuous years of the mid-1700s. Bright but rebellious, he dropped out of school while in his teens in order to join the army as a common foot soldier. In the service, he learned how advancement comes quickly in combat: during an engagement with Prussian forces, he suddenly found himself in command of a group of soldiers when a well-aimed projectile killed off all the nearby officers. The men were on the verge of fleeing, but Lamarck, by sheer lung power and force of personality, held them to their posts.

A man with such leadership ability was bound to do well in the armed forces. Had he remained in uniform, Lamarck would probably have gone down in history as a distinguished general. But an accident ended his army career abruptly and guided him, in a roundabout way, into the world of science.

Lamarck was posted to Monaco, where he injured his neck in a fight among several other officers. The damage was severe enough to mandate his early retirement, and soon Lamarck found himself looking for a new line of work.

Why not medicine? His own injury demonstrated that people are always in need of medical care, and a physician could make a good living if he chose his patients carefully. So Lamarck entered medical school. His career in medicine, however, was even briefer than his time in the army. While he was in medical school his hobby — botany — came to the attention of his friends, who persuaded him to quit the study of medicine and become a professional biologist.

Here Lamarck found his calling. He was appointed curator of a botanical garden in Paris after the French Revolution (he had had the good luck to back the winning side), and made exhaustive studies of the flora of France. Before long, his observations of living things began to make him think he could see a pattern in the development of organisms and species.

Species *did* change over time. That much seemed sure to Lamarck. Like Darwin, he had so much evidence of variation in species that he could not ignore their mutability.

Slowly but definitely, a particular plant might develop a taller stalk, or broader leaves, or gaudier petals. An animal might grow longer legs, or lose legs already developed. But *why* did these changes take place?

Lamarck decided that the environment had to be the answer. A species would not change drastically, or even subtly, without good cause; and the most likely cause, Lamarck reasoned, was a need to adapt to the environment.

A good case in point is the armor one finds on fossil fishes from the Paleozoic. Some fishes from this early age of life look like seagoing tanks, covered from nose to tail in a layer of thick bony plates, with only the tiniest openings for eyes, mouth, and anus.

The armor discouraged predators, so long as the predators were small. But when bigger predators — say, the giant lobsterlike creatures, up to nine feet long, whose fossils turn up now and then in upper New York State — appeared in the Paleozoic seas, the armored fishes faced a dilemma. Their big clawed nemeses could easily crack the fishes' bony covering, and the armor made the fishes too slow and clumsy to escape their foes.

The solution was simple. Dump the armor. And the armored fishes did exactly that. They abandoned their exterior plates and, in the process, became leaner, swifter, and more agile — and therefore much more difficult to catch.

Scenarios like this one have been repeated time and again in the history of life on earth. Some species have been forced by a change in environment — climatic upheaval, the appearance of a predator or competitor, or whatever — to either adapt or die.

Even now, the living world is in a constant state of flux, as organisms change their shapes and ways of life in order to best suit the demands of their environment. The species that can change appropriately, survive. Those that cannot, perish. And the need to adapt is constant, thought Lamarck, and so must be the process of evolution.

The important word here is "need." In Lamarck's native French, that word is *besoin*, and it has several possible meanings. Lamarck used it to mean that when species needed to change, they tended to adjust themselves, through an evolutionary process, to the demands of their environment. There was nothing outrageous about that idea. Darwin said essentially the same thing.

But because of a mistranslation, Lamarck's idea — species change because they need to change — was twisted almost beyond recognition.

The culprit was the naturalist Baron Georges Cuvier, whose reputation as a biologist and paleontologist was unsurpassed. His knowledge of comparative anatomy was so astounding that he could reconstruct an entire skeleton from a study of a single vertebra, and such feats earned him the nickname "Pope of Bones." A crusty and stodgy personality, he was never at a loss for words. Once his students decided to play a trick on him; one of them draped the hide of a stag across his back and crawled on all fours into the naturalist's bedchamber. "Cuvier, wake up!" the prankster roared in the sleeping Cuvier's ear. "I'm going to eat you!" Cuvier rolled over and found an apparition with antlers and cloven feet — strictly traits of herbivorous animals — leaning over him. He fixed the student with a basilisk stare and said, "Impossible — you have horns and hooves." Then he went back to sleep.

Cuvier read Lamarck's writings on evolutionary biology and, seeing the word *besoin*, interpreted it to mean something quite different from what Lamarck intended. *Besoin* may also mean, in certain contexts, a *decision* to do something. Cuvier attached that particular meaning to the word in Lamarck's writings, making it look as if Lamarck imagined that species *deliberately* changed themselves, then passed the alterations on to their offspring in the same way that a wealthy human passes along his or her estate to heirs. Preposterous, thought Cuvier.

Of course, Lamarck intended to say no such thing. But Cuvier's error put Lamarck's thought in a bad light among biologists, for Cuvier had tremendous prestige, and even his blunders were accepted almost as reverently as the tablets from Sinai. So Lamarck's star descended.

Lamarck suffered further at the hands of the Darwinists. The followers of Darwin, so caught up emotionally in the war of ideas between pro- and anti-evolutionists that they believed Darwin to be right and everyone else necessarily wrong, decided to make Darwin shine at Lamarck's expense. They set Lamarck up as a straw man and proceeded to knock him down, twisting Lamarck's ideas to make them appear absurd.

Transmit acquired traits? Unthinkable, sneered the Darwinists. If that were the case, then the children of sailors would be born with tattoos, and a soldier who lost a leg in battle would have to expect to beget one-legged offspring! The Darwinist attack on Lamarck was often waged on a gutter level, and was especially cowardly for being aimed at a dead man who could not respond to the charges made against him. Had Lamarck lived to face his critics in the Darwinist camp, or had Baron Cuvier interpreted Lamarck's ideas in a slightly different way, or had Lamarck expressed himself a bit more explicitly in his writings, then Lamarck might have gone down in the history of biology as a hero rather than as a laughingstock.

But a useful idea did arise, phoenixlike, from the ashes of Lamarck's reputation. For although the notion of organisms passing on acquired traits was inapplicable to the evolution of plants and animals, that concept applies perfectly to the evolution of electronic data-processing devices — which themselves are evolutionary developments of the human species, much as hands and stereo vision are.

Just how electronic computers and their data-crunching kin fit into the overall pattern of human evolution, we will see shortly.

So far, nearly everything we know about evolution of living things fits in with the Darwinian model. It is more accurate to say "neo-Darwinian," because discoveries in genetics and other branches of biology have carried evolutionary theory far beyond the relatively simple picture that Darwin originally sketched of it. For example, when Darwin was working out his theory, he was ignorant of the laws of heredity that had been discovered a few years earlier by the Austrian monk Gregor Mendel, and that explained neatly how variations arose and were transmitted. Geologists have also added considerably to our picture of biological evolution, for discoveries in paleontology and plate tectonics have revealed that evolution is not nearly the smooth and steady process that Darwin thought it to be; instead, the evolutionary progression is one of "fits and starts," with sudden occasional bursts of rapid evolution separated by long "plateaus" when not much happens. Much fine tuning remains to be done on Darwinian theory, and the years ahead may see new ideas revolutionize the science of evolution just as relativity theory revolutionized physics in the early 1900s.

As Darwin postulated, our primate ancestors appear to have followed the same general trend of evolution as many other forms of life before us, progressing from small to large, simple to complex, less intelligent to more intelligent. Our species's particular areas of specialization include upright stance, manual dexterity, and keen intellection. We are here, at the top of the primate heap, because we happen to have those traits more abundantly than the rest of the primate clan — including another human species that shared the prehistoric world with us, our late cousins the Neanderthals.

Named after the valley in Germany where their fossils were first discovered, the Neanderthals lived during the last glacial period, from about 100,000 to 40,000 years ago. They were husky hominids who stood about five feet tall, had heavy brow ridges, and were skilled in the use of stone tools. Neanderthals mastered fire and in some areas lived in caves, thus giving rise to the popular but largely inaccurate picture of Neanderthals as "cavemen." Fossils of Neanderthals have been found over wide areas of the Old World, from western Europe to Siberia to Java.

The Neanderthals have had a generally bad press in our time. Cartoonists have depicted the Neanderthal as a low-browed, chinless creature who carried a club for wooing mates, and "Neanderthal" has become a synonym for stupidity, ignorance, and bonehead conservatism. This picture seems to be wildly unjustified. Neanderthals, to judge from their fossils, were unquestionably intelligent and resourceful; indeed, their brains were slightly larger than our own. And if they were a crude people by our standards, the Neanderthals had a refined side as well; in Neanderthal graves one may find high concentrations of pollen grains, indicating that Neanderthals laid their dead to rest with flowers, just as we do.

The Neanderthals disappeared roughly 40,000 to 35,000 years ago, and their passing may have something to do with the architecture of their brains and those of their competitors, the Cro-Magnon humans, who appeared on the prehistoric scene roughly 35,000 years B.C. Cro-Magnons were, in essence, modern humans like ourselves. They stood taller than the Neanderthals (some Cro-Magnon men topped six and a half feet) and had higher foreheads. Shaved, groomed, and dressed properly, Cro-Magnons could pass for your neighbors; and in their natural state, Cro-Magnons probably looked very much like some of the young men and women one used to see walking along Haight Street in San Francisco during the Summer of Love.

What happened around 38,000 years ago, to doom the Neanderthals and give Cro-Magnons the ascendancy? It looks as if the Cro-Magnons won out over the Neanderthals for mastery of the world, because the Cro-Magnons, though their brains were smaller than those of the Neanderthals, had a little more brain tissue where it counted most: in the frontal lobes of the brain, just above the eyes. This is the part of the brain that governs imaginative thinking and deduction — what we commonly call the "smarts." And in this case a little extra intelligence seems to have counted a lot, for the Neanderthals vanish abruptly from the fossil record almost as soon as the Cro-Magnons appear on the scene. Evidently the Cro-Magnons could outthink their shorter, brutish relatives, and quickly put the Neanderthals out of business, as shown in the scenario at the opening of this chapter. A minor variation of the brain — a big little difference of a few cubic inches here and there — appears to have doomed a whole branch of humankind, and raised another to preeminence.

And now, suddenly, we find ourselves back with Oedipus. His tale may be read as an allegory of what Cro-Magnons' intelligence did for them, and consequently for us today. First it gave them mastery over the less intelligent nonhuman species, represented in the Oedipus story by the Sphinx. Once they conquered those species, they used their wits to conquer the other kinds of human life on the globe — symbolized in the Oedipus myth by the citizens of Thebes, whom Oedipus came to rule by virtue of his greater wisdom.

That is the pleasant side of the story. But what of its tragic ending? Remember, Oedipus's sharp mind led him to disaster, for the acumen that enabled him to outwit the Sphinx and that placed him on the throne of Thebes, also led him to commit a breach of morality that ultimately destroyed him. And try as he might to escape his fate, it overtook him, for his doom was foreordained. Does this part of Oedipus's history offer us a glimpse of our own condition? There is no question that human intelligence has a destructive side as well as a beneficial one, for our intellect has spawned some awful offspring: nuclear weapons depots, nerve gas repositories, and biological weapons labs all over the world. Nor is there any doubt that these horrors, if unleashed, could undo, in a few days, all the intellectual progress that humankind has made in the last few thousand years; perhaps even remove our species from the earth completely. Will our brainpower, perverted to destructive ends, demolish us in the manner of King Oedipus? And is this fate unavoidable, as was the oracle's forecast?

Let us hope not — for there is some reason for optimism. We may yet find an exit from the grisly maze in which humankind finds itself today, because the evolution of the human brain and mind has not ceased. Rather, it has taken a new and dramatic form, which, if our luck holds, may give us the wisdom and knowledge that we need to save ourselves from self-destruction.

The Wet Computer | 4

Around a table in a green-walled room stand several men and women in surgical gowns. On the table lies a young man, their patient, who is in the hospital for brain surgery.

Ordinarily a patient is put to sleep for a major operation. But in this case it is safe for him to stay awake. Indeed, the doctors need him awake, for he must respond to their questions during the operation, and his answers will guide the surgeon's fingers during the surgery.

Layer by layer, a section of the patient's head is laid open. The surgeon uses a special saw to cut through the bones of the skull, exposing several square inches of the interior to view. The next layers are part of the "life-support system" that surrounds the brain, cushioning it from jolts and supplying it with life-giving oxygen. One by one the tissues are cut through and peeled back, until the surgeon has exposed the goal of this operation: the brain itself. It is pale pink and laced with bright red blood vessels. The brain tissue gleams like lacquered porcelain under the brilliant lights of the operating theater. Looking at a living brain, one can hardly help feeling a sense of awe and perhaps a little fear as well, for in the brain lies our consciousness, our personality, our memory and intellect; in short, we are our brains, and to see a brain exposed on the operating table is to look, in a sense, at the essence of a human being.

The doctor picks up a small electric probe, somewhat similar in appearance to a soldering iron, and touches it carefully at various places to the brain's surface. "Tell me what you feel," he asks the patient.

One thing the patient does not feel is pain, for the brain itself has no pain receptors. Ironically, though the brain registers sensations from all the rest of the body, brain tissue has no sensory capability of its own; there is no need for heat receptors or pain sensors in the brain, protected as it is behind its stout wall of bone. So the patient can remain awake through this operation, conscious throughout.

But while the brain has no sensory powers within its own tissue, it does respond to stimuli from the doctor's probe. A faint electrical current goes out through the probe and into the brain tissue. And the brain answers this electrical nudge with sensations. "I feel a tingling on my wrist," says the patient. Or: "My right palm itches." Or: "My finger is burning."

Guided by these reactions, the surgeon can diagnose the problem affecting the brain, and determine what surgery is needed. A few hours later, the job is finished, the membranes are restored to the proper places, and the skull is shut. The brain, exposed so briefly to the outside world of light and cold and noise, returns to its natural capsule of darkness and warmth.

The brain is perhaps the most important organ of the body. Thanks to modern medicine, one might survive without kidneys or a stomach, and even a heart may be replaced with a man-made construction of metal and plastic; but no one can survive, under any circumstances, without a brain in reasonably good working order. The life of the brain is so closely adjoined to the life of the entire body that "brain death" — the cessation of brain activity — is accepted by many courts as proof of decease in cases where a patient on a life-support system lies in a dubious state between death and life.

The brain has many duties of which we are not normally aware. Our heartbeat and breathing are controlled in part by the brain. We could not reproduce without some information-processing functions that the brain provides. Some parts of the brain ensure that our bodies grow properly during childhood and adolescence.

And on the conscious level, the brain tells us how to recognize danger and avoid it; how to seize opportunities and make the most of them; how to plan ahead so as to make our future more secure. In short, we are our brains and what goes on inside them, for in the brain we form our images of ourselves and others, and in the brain we experience the world. And although we owe nearly everything to this organ of the body, hardly anyone except a surgeon ever *sees* a brain.

Removed from the skull, a human brain is an anticlimactic sight. It is slightly bigger than a coconut and a bit smaller than a head of cabbage. Fresh brain tissue is pink; after death it fades to yellow-gray. Until it starts decaying, it has no smell. In texture, the brain is only marginally firmer than gravy. Because of its high water content (the brain is the most watery tissue of the body, except for the blood), the brain, outside the skull, cannot support its own weight. Place a freshly removed brain on a table, and the organ will sag and ooze outward to the sides. Squeeze a bit of brain tissue between your fingers, and it will feel like a gelatin dessert not quite yet jelled.

One of the brain's most dramatic features, to the casual observer, is its convoluted surface. The outermost layer, or cortex, of the brain, is wrinkled and folded into a complex pattern of ridges and valleys, like a contour map of a watershed. The creases in the cortex are a clever packaging technique on the part of nature. Rather than increase the size of the skull in direct proportion to the increase in cortical volume — an approach that might have given humans heads too big to manage easily — the process of natural selection folded and crumpled the cortex so that a lot of extra brain tissue could be squeezed into the skull. Just as you fold clothes carefully before putting them in a suitcase, the fabric of the cortex was convoluted to take full advantage of every last cubic inch of room within the head.

Brains vary little in appearance. If you have seen one brain, you have seen nearly all of them. Isaac Newton's brain probably looked no different from Joe Smith's or your own. Brain size may differ from one individual to another; Ivan Turgenev and Oliver Cromwell are said to have had extremely large brains, for example, while Emile Zola reportedly had a very small one. But otherwise, on a gross anatomical level, a brain is a brain is a brain.

On finer levels of organization and structure, the mysteries of the brain are even greater than those of the planet Pluto's surface. Let us start with a look at the smallest unit of the brain, the individual nerve cell, or *neuron*.

The neurons are not the only kind of cell in the brain; some of the approximately 100 billion cells in the average-sized human brain (by comparison, there are only about four billion human beings on earth) are supporting cells, an organic scaffolding of sorts that keeps the brain more or less in its given shape and prevents it from disintegrating into a disorganized cellular mush. But the neurons are the cells that keep the brain in business.

A representative neuron has a roughly spherical or pyramidal cell body studded with dozens or even hundreds of long slender projections called *dendrites,* which extend out in all directions from it like the branches of a tree or shrub. One other projection is much longer than the dendrites, and is called the *axon*. It looks somewhat like a long chain of frankfurters. The axon consists of a nerve fiber surrounded by an insulating sheath of a substance called *myelin*. The axon is divided into its sausage portions by small breaks in the myelin sheath, known as the *nodes of Ranvier*. How these nodes operate, we will see in a moment.

As a rule, the axon is very long in proportion to the cell body. Loft a kite several hundred feet up into the air; imagine the kite to be the cell body and the string to be the axon, and you will have a good idea of their relative dimensions. Axons more than a foot in length are not uncommon in the human body, and some are as long as your arm. At the very end, the axon branches out into a treelike network of terminal fibers, which touch neighboring cells and pass along signals to them.

These bizarre-looking cells are remarkable in many ways, not least because they have lost the power to reproduce themselves. The other cells of the body can divide and replace themselves as they wear out and die, but the nerve cells lose this trait before the fetus comes out of the womb. Their inability to divide means that each of us is born with all the neurons that she or he will ever possess.*

The living neuron is a fantastically complex phenomenon. It owes its function to electrochemistry. Though the nerve impulse is an electrical signal, it passes from cell to cell with the help of chemicals.

Here is an illustration. You are looking right now at a set of dark marks on paper. This pattern of black-on-white symbols reaches your eyes by reflected light, and activates the nerve cells in the retina, the light-sensing layer of nerve cells at the back of your eyeball. The result is a set of nerve impulses, which are transferred to your brain's vision centers for processing. The signal is passed along from cell to cell on the way to the brain, like the baton in a relay race, and as the impulse sweeps by, a complex electrochemical transfer takes place.

Inside the nerve cell, fluids are relatively rich in potassium ions (the word *ion* means that the atom has an electrical charge), while outside the cell there is a much higher concentration of sodium ions. The nerve cell maintains this disequilibrium with the help of an "ion pump," which ushers excess sodium atoms out of the cell and pumps in enough potassium from the external fluid to keep the potassium/sodium balance lopsided. Why is this imbalance necessary? Because it helps send the nerve impulse on its way.

Set all along the axon are protein molecules called *potassium gates* and *sodium gates*. Each one passes its particular kind of ion in or out of the cell. As the nerve impulse sweeps by them, the sodium and potassium gates open in sequence, first allowing sodium to enter, and then potassium to escape, altering the electrical potential of the membrane and moving the electrical impulse along. This process takes place at the nodes of Ranvier, which are the only spots along the axon where the cell membrane actually comes in contact with the

---

* Neurons are not responsible for tumors of the brain, in which brain cells start dividing abnormally fast and create lumpy growths of tissue that press on the surrounding neurons and may cause abnormal behavior. Supporting cells are responsible for turmors; or, alternatively, tumors may be transported to the brain from other organs via the bloodstream, which can carry cancerous cells all over the body from the site of origin. This process is called metastasis.

external fluids; and so the nodes of Ranvier might be visualized as boosters for the nerve signal.

At the end of the axon, the nerve impulse faces a hurdle: how to jump the gap between the terminal fibers of the axon to the tips of the dendrites of the closest neuron, where another axon connects. The space is about five billionths of an inch — minuscule by everyday standards, but still a formidable chasm for something the size of an atom or molecule.

The impulse goes through by means of a mechanism known as a *synapse.* At the very tip, each terminal fiber on the axon bulges out into a shape like that of a doorknob. This bulge is full of tiny sacs called *vesicles,* each one full of special chemicals, *neurotransmitters,* which squirt out from the axon's terminal branch and leap the gap between it and the dendrites of the adjacent cell.

All of this happens so quickly, even along a string of several dozen cells, that you perceive it as an instantaneous process. Actually, nerve impulses travel rather slowly compared to other phenomena of nature. If you could pinch a brontosaur's tail and, at the same moment, fire an artillery shell from his tail toward his head, the shell would whiz past his nose before the nerve impulse could reach his rump.

Not only does the axon interface with the dendrites, but the dendrites branch out and interconnect with one another as well, forming a vastly intricate tracery of nerve cells that makes a big-city phone system look crude by comparison. One can get some idea of the complexity of the brain by looking at slides of brain tissue that have been stained by a special process, known as the Golgi stain, which colors only one cell in a hundred or so, and leaves the rest unaffected. (The Golgi stain has been in use for more than a century, but still we have no idea why it works in this highly selective way.) Here and there a stained nerve cell stands out boldly, its cell body the focus of dozens of dark traces of dendrites, like the plumes of fire from a Fourth of July skyrocket. A bit farther away, another neuron flings out a burst of dendrites, and nearby still another does the same. Now fill in with your imagination all the other, unstained cells, perhaps 99 percent of the total that also reside in this slice of brain.

Each cell makes hundreds of dendritic contacts, and there are a hundred billion cells in the brain. This kind of complexity is more than most brains can envision. Imagine each person on earth, making perhaps 100,000 telephone calls per day, every day, even in sleep, and you have some notion of the activity that goes on inside your own skull.

In recent years we have greatly expanded our understanding of how the neurons "talk" to one another. The classical theory of nerve-cell communication went roughly as follows. Nerve impulses followed a single, clear-cut pathway of transmission, from the cell body of a neuron, down the axon to the terminal fibers, across the gap to the dendrites of the next cell, at which point the process starts over again. Cell to axon to dendrites to cell to axon to dendrites . . . and so on. This Tinker-to-Evers-to-Chance model was once compared to a corporate board meeting. The various board members correspond to the dendrites; they offer input in the form of facts and opinions, for the consideration of the entire board, which here represents the nerve cell as a whole. J. B., the chairman, here stands for the axon. When the output is ready ("All right, we buy Consolidated!"), he picks up the phone, and delivers the message to whomever it may concern. In this case all the other corporate boards on earth might be compared to all the other cells of the brain. Some are linked directly, others in a more roundabout manner; but all the boards are part of a free-market economy, just as all the neurons are elements of the brain.

Biologists have a long-standing habit of borrowing models from economics to explain the workings of the natural world. Darwin, for example, lifted many concepts from the followers of Adam Smith, especially when he was dealing with the role of competition and natural selection in evolution. Unfortunately, this habit has often led biologists to draw wrong conclusions, because economic models tend to be highly oversimplified. Darwin's fondness for this way of thinking led him astray on occasion, and similarly the board-meeting model of nerve function turned out to be unrealistic. The dendrites turned out to be quite a bit more than a mere input system for signals transferred down the axon. Now it is known that the dendrites carry out a surprising amount of chatter among themselves, and are not dependent on the axon to be their mouthpiece (so to speak). This discovery raised estimates of the brain's complexity by several orders of magnitude, and brain researchers can hardly be blamed if they feel despair at the size of the tasks before them, since every mystery they solve concerning the brain's operation seems to create a hundred mysteries more.

So much for individual nerve cells. How do their input and output affect the nervous system as a whole?

Our input, generally speaking, is the evidence of our senses: sight, sound, touch, taste, smell. Our output is our vastly complicated set of responses to our perceptions of the world around us. The sensation of heat from touching a candle flame is input. The cry of "Ouch!" and the quick withdrawal of the hand are output. And somewhere in between these two extremes is a huge, shadowy range of mental operations, about some of which we barely know more than their names: memory, intuition, decision.

Most happenings in the brain are so complicated, involving so many neurons in such a bewildering mass of information exchanges, that the processes defy all understanding. Not only does the complexity of the thinking brain defeat most efforts to study its operations, but also its speed makes such studies difficult. Signals flit from one neuron to another so rapidly that even the most sophisticated equipment, under the most carefully controlled conditions in a laboratory, can barely intercept and interpret them.

What we have learned about the more subtle processes of the brain is flabbergasting. A small example has to do with vision. Look around you, and you will see your surroundings in a continuous field of view. When you think about it, this is odd, because the anatomy of your eye suggests there should be a little hole right in the middle of your vision, caused by the "blind spot" in the eye. This is a spot on the retina where no nerve cells are located — the point where nerve fibers converge to enter the optic nerve running to the brain. Since no information is picked up at the blind spot, you might expect to go through life peering around a small blob of nonvision right in the middle of your vista. But you don't. Why not?

Together, the brain and eyes perform a trick of information processing to make you forget that the blind spot is there. They fill in the missing information from that corner of the retina. The blind spot is not large, and your nervous system can easily figure out, subconsciously, what ought to be in that part of your view, on the basis of what you see immediately around the blind spot. So you are ordinarily unconscious of this little lacuna in your sight; it becomes evident only under very special conditions, such as the familiar nose-touching trick you used to perform in grade school.

Another of the mysterious and wonderful processes at work in the brain is "false memory." Contrary to popular belief, human memory is not merely a process of taking in data and storing them in the head for future reference. The memory mechanism is so much more complicated — and deceptive — that our traditional concept of memory is starting to look slightly shaky.

Police departments have to deal frequently with the phenomenon of false memory. Scenes like the following are not uncommon in precincts around the country:

Sergeant Brown is assigned to Homicide, and one of his cases involves a man who walked into a restaurant one night, pumped six shots from a revolver into another man, seated at a front table, and then fled into the darkness outside. The sergeant asks three persons present at the restaurant that night to describe the killer.

Mr. Jones, a waiter, answers first. "He was about six feet tall, Caucasian, with straight black hair, and weighed about one hundred seventy-five pounds."

But Mr. Perkins, a bookkeeper who caught a glimpse of the gunman that night, remembers quite a different image of him: "He was a Latino, I think, about five-ten, with a mustache."

And Mrs. Barker, a waitress, gives still another contradictory description: "I thought he was Oriental or Oriental-American."

At this point Sergeant Brown understands why very few murder cases get solved in this country. Fortunately for the police, the killer feels the pangs of conscience and turns himself in. Looking at the accused murderer's photo, Brown sees that the waiter's description was essentially right. The culprit stands about six feet tall, and has pale skin and straight black hair. He is also clean-shaven. Why, then, did the three witnesses give such wildly varying accounts of his appearance?

Here we see how the brain operates. The witnesses knew they would be asked to describe the killer, but except for the waiter, they had only the sketchiest recollection of what the gunman looked like. They had heard the shots, turned to see what was happening, and caught only the briefest glimpse of him before he ran out the door and was gone. So the witnesses' imaginations went to work creating false memories to fill in the picture of the assailant. Deep in the bookkeeper's mind, the black hair of the killer stirred a half-forgotten memory of a Latino villain in a TV movie; without fully realizing where that image came from, Mr. Perkins projected it onto the murderer and went to the police station convinced that this phony memory was what he had really seen. Mrs. Barker, on the other hand, had just finished reading a thriller about the Yakuza, the Japanese gangster fraternity, and a picture of gun-toting modern-day samurai was still fresh in her mind. So, understandably, she reconstructed the killer along the lines of an Oriental-American. All three witnesses were convinced their impressions were accurate, yet only one description of the gunman fitted him.

False memory accounts for much of popular culture. The American nostalgia for high school is based to a large extent on falsified memories; most Americans in their thirties recall high school as a time of blessed unconcern, when in fact the records of high school counselors indicate it is almost always a painful period for the student, when one has most of an adult's responsibilities but very few of an adult's rights and privileges.

Indeed, false memory seems to account for so much of our thinking that one naturally has to wonder: how much of what we know is really accurate? Some of our stored information — say, Newton's law of gravitation — can be proven correct by experiment. What goes up obviously must come down. But many other memories are so phantasmagoric that we sometimes seem to be walking around in a cloud of illusion (an idea to which we will return in the next chapter). Can we be sure of *anything* we know? Michel de Montaigne considered that question several centuries ago, and decided the answer was no. Today many brain researchers and psychologists are inclined to agree with him. The deep and dark currents of brain activity seem to be rearranging our memories all the time, like bits of driftwood in the sea.

Then there is the strange sorting process by which the three-pound blob of soggy tissue in your head surveys the many bits of information pouring upward into your mind, and ranks them according to their importance.

As you read this page, the eyes and brain are taking in information that you consider important enough to merit your full attention. This information has priority at the moment. But at the same time, the rest of your sensory apparatus is far from idle. Nerve cells in your skin are reporting on your immediate environment, telling you whether your surroundings are hot or cold, moist or dry, calm or windy. Impulses from these cells — which are known technically as *transducers,* the name for any receptor that turns information into electrical impulses — are streaming along nerves to your spinal column, and from there upward to the brain.

Your ears are picking up sounds. Olfactory cells in your nose are detecting smells. Possibly you are sipping tea or coffee, and taste buds on your tongue are conveying the flavor of your drink to the brain along with all the rest of this torrent of incoming information.

Half heard and half felt are all the little mechanical operations of the body, too: the thump of the heart, the whoosh of the lungs, the faint pop of a wrist bone as you turn a page. All of it goes to the brain; all of it is sensed somewhere in that double handful of pink tissue.

There is much more information coming in than your conscious mind can juggle. If you had to pay equal attention to everything you sensed, you might die — or perhaps go mad — from information overload. So the brain sorts through all the incoming signals, and lets them through to your conscious mind in order of importance. Only the very important bits of information will get through to your conscious thoughts. You can afford to ignore the steady repetitive noise of a normally working heart; but let a sharp pain shoot through the left side of your chest, and suddenly your consciousness is alert to it. *Heart attack?* you wonder.

All at once you are keenly aware of other, usually ignored, sensations that the brain has just reclassified as vitally important. Difficulty in breathing? Faintness? Pains spreading to the arm? Quickly you review the list of symptoms. If you are lucky, none of them appear. Whew: must not be a heart attack after all — more likely just a muscle pain. But better see a doctor as soon as possible, to be safe.

How the brain achieves such feats of communication and association, we have only the vaguest idea. The inner workings of the brain are less familiar to us than the bottom of the sea or the geology of the moon. If one takes the word *mind* to stand for the brain's operation, then what Percy Bysshe Shelley wrote in 1815 still holds true: "The caverns of the mind are obscure and shadowy, or pervaded with a luster, beautifully bright indeed, but shining not beyond their portals."

Still, we do know, in a very general way, where certain parts of the mind are anchored, and it is possible to divide the contents of our heads into three more or less separate brains and minds.

If you could slice a brain longitudinally in half, you would see a set of concentric structures like those in a rose or cabbage. In the center is a lumpy mass of tissue, about the size of a lemon, growing out of the upper end of the spinal cord. Anatomists call it the *archipallium*. It is more commonly known as the "reptilian brain" or the "R-complex," and is our heritage from the days of the dinosaurs. The main concern of the reptiles was, and is, mere survival, and for that purpose a brain with rather simple "programming" is sufficient. Much of the reptiles' behavior is preprogrammed into them before birth, and consists of information needed to give the individual — and therefore the species — the best chance of surviving. In the reptilian mind, it pays to assume that anyone and everyone much different from you, and not obviously prey, is an enemy to be either shunned or destroyed. If a creature does look like fair game, then by all means attack it and gobble it down. And above all else, stake out some territory for yourself and defend it; otherwise you may find yourself out in the cold, cruel world without a home. These three articles of faith, and a few others equally cold-blooded in nature, comprise what might be called the Reptiles' Creed. When our distant reptilian ancestors evolved into the more intelligent, bigger-brained mammals, that creed was never erased. For reasons we will see shortly, it lurked in the depths of the mammalian mind, and is still part of the mammals' psyches — including our own.

The reptilian mind is, in a sense, the dark side of the human character. Your reptilian mind is what tells you to cheat your friends, rob the cash drawer, look out for Number One, and to hell with everyone else. From this deeply buried repository of ancient drives and instincts bubble up many of the motives that bring tragedy to the world: aggression, territoriality, and xenophobia, to name only three.

Adolf Hitler's policies as chancellor of Germany came very close to summarizing the goals of the reptilian mind. In Hitler's Germany, xenophobia took the form of anti-Semitism and a twisted "racial consciousness." The Nazis' military aims were largely territorial; Hitler sought to conquer all Europe on the excuse of providing more *Lebensraum* (living space) for the German people. And when the Nazi leaders sent tanks rolling across the border into Poland, their aggressive policy was flowing directly up from the reptile brain.

Lest we think the reptilian mind has some special hold on Germans, we ought to take a close look at our own nation's history, for reptilian-style thinking has colored the life of the Republic for more than two centuries — colored it bloodred in many cases. When the first European settlers to reach New England waged genocidal war against the native Americans, the reptilian brain was behind the slaughter. The anti-immigration groups of the 1800s, such as the Know-Nothings, spoke for the reptilian mind when they worked for the closing of our doors to foreigners. And in our own century the reptilian level of the brain has spawned any number of hate groups, from racist societies to fanatical nationalists (such as the Hundred Percenters of the First World War).

But the reptilian mind is only one part of the whole. The next step up from the reptile brain is the *paleopallium,* or "old mammalian brain." This set of structures is wrapped around the reptilian brain and represents what the early mammals developed during and shortly after the dinosaurs' decline. Rather than revamp the brain completely, another layer was added to the already existing reptilian brain. Since the old mammalian brain developed from the centers that govern smell, it is also sometimes known as the "smell brain." Another common name for it is the "limbic system."

The limbic system handles many duties, but one of the most important things it supplies is emotion. When we cry at the movies, or cheer at a football game, the limbic system is speaking out. This is the part of the brain that brought Romeo to Juliet, sent Childe Harold on his pilgrimage, and motivated Augustine to repent of his sins. Hate and love, hope and fear, elation and despair all have their origins here, in a mass of tissue about the size of a large apple. Sitting atop the reptilian mind, the old mammalian mind usually dominates it and can overrule it; the emotion of love, for example, can drown out the insistent voice of self-interest that hisses constantly from the reptilian brain. The soldier who throws himself on a grenade to save his comrades from the blast is a vivid testimonial to the power of the limbic system.

But the programming of the limbic system is so powerful that it must have some checks on it, or else the mind would be driven by blind emotion. So the old mammalian mind is tempered, one might say, by a still higher level of the mind: the "neomammalian mind," which is centered in the outer layer of the brain, known as the cerebral cortex, or *neopallium*. Here the highest functions of the mind take place. This is what we commonly call the "thinking mind." It is the logical, methodical, most highly organized part of the mind, the part that comes into play when you read a book, or work a crossword puzzle. Here arose what we consider to be the achievements of civilization, from the United Nations to the detective story. This uppermost, thinking mind is the element of us that tries to make sense of the world. It is the side of us that appreciates beauty, brings order out of chaos, and keeps us from sliding back to the life-style of our remote simian ancestors. All this, carried out by only a pound or so of nerve tissue.

Three minds in one: the triune human brain is a fairly new concept among scientists, but we can see it represented all through literature, religion, and philosophy. Arthur Conan Doyle's stories of Sherlock Holmes, for example, dramatize the cooperation — and conflict — among these three levels of the mind. Holmes, the master detective, with his keen sense of deductive reasoning, stands for the neomammalian mind, the quick-thinking part of us. Holmes's nemesis is Professor Moriarty, the cold-blooded master criminal whose interests are basically those of the reptilian mind: power and survival. And in between these two opposed figures stands Dr. Watson, Holmes's friend and confidant, a sturdy soul with a warm heart and a quick temper, but not too much in the way of brains — the embodiment, in short, of the old mammalian mind. Together, Holmes and Watson put an end to Moriarty, just as the two higher levels of the human mind keep the reptilian mind from breaking out. And whenever a conflict occurs between Watson and Holmes, the latter almost invariably wins out, in the manner of the neomammalian mind dominating the old mammalian mind.

But what of the times when reason fails, and the underside of the mind breaks loose? Robert Louis Stevenson dramatized that situation in his novel *Dr. Jekyll and Mr. Hyde*, in which the highly civilized and humane Dr. Jekyll concocts a potion that transforms him into his own evil alter ego, the malignant and brutal Mr. Hyde. (Fredric March, in the 1932 film version of Stevenson's story, made the release of the doctor's "animal" mind especially vivid; his makeup made Hyde actually look subhuman, like something out of the late Mesozoic.) Dracula and the Wolf Man are other famous variations on this theme: havoc results whenever the guiding force of our neomammalian mind breaks down.

If you turn on a car radio while driving through the Deep South, you are likely to hear the conflict among the various levels of the mind expressed in terms like these: "You are sinners! All have sinned and come short of the glory of God! You are in bondage to that great serpent, the Devil! But Jesus will save you! Put your trust in Him! Praise the Lord! He will lead the righteous to salvation!"

The evil and sinful side of humankind corresponds roughly to the reptilian mind, while righteousness is a fair description of what goes on in the neomammalian mind — an endless struggle to keep the lid on our prehistoric urges and instincts. Salvation here is that blessed state where the sinful reptilian side of the human mind is confined forever, powerless to vex the world again. Christ symbolizes the highest and noblest portions of the neomammalian mind, and the Devil embodies our intellectual baggage left over from the age of reptiles. (As various commentators have pointed out, it is probably no accident that the Devil is so often portrayed, in Scripture and in art, as a snake, dragon, or other winged lizard.)

The cerebral cortex and the "thinking" mind it houses made it possible for humans to rise above the level of the reptiles and lower mammals, and take over the world. But ironically, after this part of our brain and mind evolved, humans found themselves at a dead end of sorts. They had packed about as much thinking power as possible into the limited volume of their heads. Within the confines of the extant brain, there was nowhere left to go, no place to slip in much more brain tissue for increased thinking capacity. The human mind was in much the same position as a large family that has outgrown its present house and needs more living space, but cannot locate a bigger house to move into. In a case like that, the family would probably add a new room or two onto their home. Could humans do the same thing with their brains and minds?

Not exactly. There is no practical way to build an extra room onto the skull and pour in a few extra ounces of brain tissue to beef up one's mind. But one *could* build a surrogate mind, so to speak — a mental annex where devices could handle some functions of the mind for us, and free our minds for other labors. How that annex came to be is one of the most exciting stories in the history of science and technology.

Up from Fingers | 5

Climbing a tree, throwing a rock, figuring the best spot to set a trap for game: at these jobs the three-pound computer inside the skull was superb. The proof of its effectiveness was the rapid ascendancy of *Homo sapiens.* In less than 100,000 years — a mere instant on the scale of geologic time — the human intellect made its owners the masters of the planet.

No other species could associate or remember facts as well as humans could. Therefore, no other species could accomplish such feats as the taming of fire and the making of sophisticated tools.*

To put it another way, humans could use their big brains to *extend* themselves. We are the extended animal. We can build extensions of ourselves to do what our bodies cannot. Where our hands and arms cannot reach, we can build remote-control devices to handle things for us. To carry deadly force beyond arm's reach, we have spears and arrows, missiles and laser beams. Television is an extension of the human eye and ear. Radar is an extension of our sight. Automobiles

---

* The key word here is sophisticated, because ours is not the only species to use tools. Chimpanzees, as noted earlier, use twigs as probes when seeking insects in logs and the soil, and even certain birds drop rocks on eggs of other birds in order to break them open for food.

and aircraft are extensions of our limbs, carrying us where muscle power alone cannot.

With the help of their extensions — cutting tools, the plow, and so forth — humans quickly rose above the level of mere predators, and developed the highly organized, agriculture-based way of life we know as civilization.

On the whole, civilization was a blessing. It allowed us to specialize into different jobs and professions: farmer, blacksmith, physician, and so forth. And with this division of labor came increased prosperity, for the specialists could then take time to do their jobs as well as possible — for the benefit of the whole community.

But civilization also brought with it a problem. It involved keeping track of property. As civilization became ever more organized, humans had to keep records of their belongings more accurately than before. It was no longer adequate to say, "Our tribe's territory starts at the edge of this valley and includes the whole valley and the lake beyond." Now it was necessary to say, "My land starts *exactly* here, and your land starts *precisely* there" — down to the very inch if possible. Farmers in the vicinity of the Nile, for example, were competing for every last bit of arable land and so had to know the boundaries of their lands precisely, or else risk losing productivity to a neighbor. Merchants had to know the size of their inventories to the last item. Bankers — or their equivalents — were well-advised to know where every last coin was, on pain of losing money. On a slightly higher level, priests monitoring the motions of celestial bodies needed to be able to tell how far Mars or the moon had moved in a given time; otherwise, forecasts made on the basis of the planets' progress would be worthless.

This kind of mental effort was much more than the human mind originally had to handle. To a Cro-Magnon tribesman in neolithic France, anything over ten or twenty, the total of his digits, was probably just "many." (Among some South American native tribes today, there is no word for numbers higher than five.) And for many centuries that kind of primitive arithmetic was sufficient.

But a civilized society required more sophisticated ways of handling numbers. And so humans had to extend not their bodies, but

their *minds,* to increase their information-processing power. Therefore, the first computers were invented, to extend the limited mathematical abilities of our minds.

Several civilizations developed simple computing devices early in
their histories. The Orientals had the famous abacus, which until the
mid-twentieth century remained unsurpassed in speed and accuracy
when in the hands of a well-trained operator.

The Incas of Peru had the *quipu,* a set of knotted ropes reminiscent of a cat-o'-nine-tails. Knots in the ropes stood for numerical
measurements. The keeper of the quipu was the Inca equivalent of a
CPA, and one can only wonder if he, like some of his modern colleagues, felt the urge to practice "creative accounting" now and
then, slipping a knot here and there, and then slipping some ill-got-
ten money into his purse. Auditing a quipu-keeper must have been
like straightening out a tangled fishing line.

The Roman "pocket calculator" was the human hand. Beset by a
highly cumbersome system of numerals, Romans had to rely on a
complicated system of finger arithmetic to do their sums. In Caesar's
day, unlike ours, counting on one's fingers was a sign of advanced
education and skill.

Even with calculating aids, however, arithmetic must have posed
fearsome problems for the Romans. Imagine trying to multiply
MMMCCCCLVIII (in our numerals, 3,458) times CCCCLIX (459).

The so-called Arabic system of numerals that we use today (it actually originated in India) simplified math greatly when it was introduced to Europe, because the Arabic concept of place value — in
which one column stands for ones, the next column for tens, the next
for hundreds, and so forth — eliminated the need to juggle all those
Roman M's, C's, and the rest. Using the Arabic system, a mathematician with pen and paper could carry out the multiplication problem in
the previous paragraph in perhaps thirty seconds; a Roman wiggling
his fingers might require ten minutes.

But calculation remained a time-consuming nuisance. Moreover,
the longer and more complex the calculation, the more one risked
making a mistake. Even a seemingly little error, such as an incorrect
numeral in the tens column, could mean disaster; by that kind of
mistake, a clumsy navigator might guide his ship to destruction on

the rocks instead of to a safe harbor. (Indeed, many shipwrecks in the eighteenth and nineteenth centuries were caused by seamen relying on navigational tables that had been figured incorrectly.)

There was a tremendous need, then, for faster and more reliable ways to calculate. Mathematicians especially were eager for better computing tools, because their science was expanding faster than the technology of handling numbers. By the time Renaissance mathematicians were enlarging the realms of geometry, algebra, and number theory, the need for fast and accurate long calculations was becoming acute. Was there no way to avoid the drudgery of calculating?

Perhaps there was. The Renaissance was an age of machinery, and engineers of that time had designed and built gadgets to take over many unpleasant and time-consuming jobs from humans — grinding grain and hauling water, to name only two examples. Could machines also be designed to carry out long, exacting calculations automatically, and thus free humans for more productive labor?

One of the first inventors to tackle this project was a seventeenth-century German named Wilhelm Schickard. A professor of mathematics and astronomy, and a friend of the famous astronomer Johannes Kepler, Schickard appears to have succeeded in building a mechanical calculator that could add, subtract, multiply, and divide numbers well into the hundreds: a prodigious feat for the day.

Schickard planned to send Kepler one of his marvelous machines, but luck was against the inventor. In 1624, a fire broke out at the workshop where the calculator was being assembled, and the device was destroyed. The local metalworker, who had built it to Schickard's specifications, had no time to rebuild it. Eventually a copy was reconstructed from Schickard's notes, but by that time Schickard was dead, a victim of pestilence spread by troop movements during the Thirty Years' War. This string of unfortunate events was a tremendous loss for science; had Schickard been able to introduce his calculator to the scientific community in the early seventeenth century, science and technology might have taken a giant leap forward, and knowledge still undreamed of might be ours today.

Better luck was with the next man to try building a mechanical calculator, the French mathematician and philosopher Blaise Pascal.

Perhaps "man" is not quite the proper word to describe him, because Pascal spent much of his life trying to be more than human, and ended up less a man than a monster.

Born in 1623 into a prosperous family, Pascal showed mathematical genius while still at kindergarten age. Before reaching puberty he had reportedly worked out all the geometrical axioms of Euclid for himself, in exactly the same order as Euclid had. (How many of the tales about Pascal's early years are true, it is difficult to say; his family was the source for many of them, and proud relatives are prone to exaggerate.)

Pascal's greatest achievement was a branch of math called probability theory. Next to calculus, probability is the most important kind of math in use today, for it helps us separate the *likely* from the merely *possible*.

A high-living friend gave Pascal the germ of his theory. One day Pascal was traveling with the Chevalier de Méré, a minor nobleman with a love of worldly pleasures, such as games of chance. The trip was long, the road was dusty, and the carriage was miserably uncomfortable; these were the days before coil-spring seat cushions, and the human behind tended to tire after a couple of hours on the hard wood seats of a carriage.

To take their minds off the miseries of travel, Méré put a problem to Pascal. How, asked Méré, does one split the pot in an interrupted dice game, when neither player has an opportunity to finish the game and win the whole amount?

Pascal mused on the problem. The split, he decided, must be made according to which player stood the better chance of winning when the game was halted. The player more likely to have won deserves the greater share of the money, and the other player the lesser share. But how should one put a numerical value on the chance of one player winning and the other losing?

Pascal decided he needed help, and he called in his mathematician colleague Pierre de Fermat, a jurist who dabbled in math as a hobby. The two men exchanged letters for several years, working out the mathematical basis of probability.

Without probability theory, the world as we know it would not exist, for probability calculations govern hundreds of things we do daily. When we buy products at the store, the pills or canned foods or whatever have been probability-tested to make sure that the vast majority of individual items are safe and sound. Your life insurance premiums are figured on the basis of probability: that is, how likely you are to die in any given year of your life. Part of the electricity that runs appliances in your home comes from nuclear power stations; and there probably would be no such stations if physicists had not had probability theory to help unlock the inner secrets of the atom. Every time probability theory touches your life, you are in debt to Blaise Pascal.

Undeniably, Pascal was a genius. Unfortunately, he was also mad for much of his life. John Dryden might have been thinking of Pascal when he wrote:

> Great wits are sure to madness near allied,
> And thin partitions do their bounds divide.

No mind had thinner partitions than Pascal's.

But Pascal's madness could not silence his mighty mathematical mind. Even in his wildest moments, he was still thinking math. Once, he used probability theory to describe the wages of faith and unbelief. If you accept Christ as your savior, Pascal argued, and the claims of the Bible turn out to be false, then you have lost nothing of importance. But if you reject Christ, and the Bible turns out to be telling the truth, then you have virtually no chance of escaping damnation. On the other hand, if you follow the Lord and the Biblical message is true, then your probability of attaining heaven and escaping hell is virtually 100 percent.*

One thing bothered Pascal almost as much as the sinful state of humankind: the labors of calculation. Even fairly simple math problems involved long minutes or hours, and sometimes days, of effort with pencil and paper. The hand cramped, the back ached, and the

---

* This gambling analogy offended many of Pascal's fellow Christians, who objected to his describing salvation in terms of a dice game. Even the agnostic Voltaire thought Pascal's reasoning "did not befit the gravity of the subject."

eyes burned after long periods hunched over a desk, scribbling figures. So Pascal decided to try speeding the process by mechanical means.

Pascal's time was the heyday of clockwork gadgetry. Every day craftsmen were coming up with new mechanical novelties to amuse the upper classes. The king of France was especially fond of a windup toy invented for his dinner parties; it consisted of a sculpture of the god Neptune riding a sea turtle. Wound up and placed on the table after meals, the turtle would lumber from place to place, dispensing toothpicks while Neptune prodded the beast along with his trident.

But the royal toy was a frivolous use of machinery. Pascal thought a mechanism could be put to much more productive use as a calculator. So he sat down at his desk and designed a device he called the *arithmétique.* It consisted of a brass box about the size of a loaf of bread, with eight dials on its face. Using a stylus to turn the dials, one could enter onto each of them numbers in a given column: hundredths, tenths, and so forth, up to the hundreds of thousands.

Pascal's machine was less sophisticated than Schickard's and could only add and subtract. Moreover, the *arithmétique* was so expensive that no one wanted to buy it. For the price of Pascal's invention one could hire a whole townful of mathematicians for a job, and another whole townful to check their work for accuracy.

Consequently, economics doomed Pascal's plan. His calculator went onto the shelf, and Pascal went on to insanity and to fame as a philosopher.

About three decades after Pascal introduced his *arithmétique,* another philosopher-mathematician, Gottfried Wilhelm Leibniz, tried his hand at building a calculating machine. Leibniz is best remembered as the co-inventor of calculus. He conceived that powerful tool of mathematics at roughly the same time as his rival, Sir Isaac Newton, and neither man ever quite forgave the other for stealing part of the credit. (The personal rivalry between the two men spilled over into the writings of their followers, with sometimes absurd results. For example, Newton used a lowercase "d" in writing out differentials, whereas Leibniz used a small dot for that purpose; and for many years afterward a debate raged over the merits of Leibniz's "dotism" versus the "pure d-ism" of Newton — a pun on Newton's religious beliefs.) Once, Leibniz, hoping to defeat Newton, posed a fiendishly difficult problem. It involved calculating the area underneath a curve swept out by a bead sliding down a thread. The puzzle reached Newton, and he dashed off a solution one evening after coming home from his government job as director of the mint. The answer was not credited to Newton, but when Leibniz saw it, he knew whose work it was. "I recognize the lion by his paw," Leibniz said.

When Leibniz turned his attention to the mysteries of the mind, especially the riddle of perception, he reached a mind-shaking conclusion. We have, he said, no way of knowing for sure that anything we perceive is real!

Our lives might be complete illusions, according to Leibniz — and we would never know it if the illusions were self-consistent. Would the *illusions* then be real? "I should think [them] real enough," said Leibniz. (A few hundred years later, researchers trying to unravel the problems of perception and intelligence would rediscover, to their own dismay, just how truly Leibniz had spoken. And when the Beatles, about the same time, sang that nothing was real, they were borrowing a thought from the co-inventor of calculus.)

Whether life was real or illusory, Leibniz dreamed of reducing it to a kind of calculus, a mathematical system that could be used to analyze human behavior. Leibniz himself never came close to such a mathematical synthesis of existence, but in the twentieth century another mathematician, John von Neumann, would originate a branch of math very close to what Leibniz had in mind; von Neumann's work will be the topic of a later chapter.

Leibniz, as much as anyone else, hated the tedium of calculating, and longed for some way to speed up the process. "It is unworthy of excellent men," he grumbled, "to lose hours like slaves in the labor of calculation that could be safely relegated to anyone else if machines were used."

He therefore created a calculator more advanced than Pascal's, the "Leibniz wheel." It looked like a cross between a slide rule and an old-fashioned meat grinder, but it worked, and could handle multiplication and division, as well as addition and subtraction. But Leibniz was fated to disappointment, just as Pascal had been, for the Leibniz wheel failed to revolutionize math. It was still too costly for any but the richest individual, and too limited in its capabilities to give mathematicians more than minor aid. Thanks in part to Leibniz's own work on calculus, mathematicians now routinely had to work out calculations far beyond the powers of any then-existing machines, including the Leibniz wheel.

Leibniz died in 1716, neglected by his countrymen and outshone in genius by Newton. The only person to show up for Leibniz's funeral was his private secretary. But Leibniz's work bore fruit long after his death. His machine inspired other designers to work on refining calculating machines, and one by one the advancements appeared that would lead at last to the computers of today.

The next step forward in the evolution of computers came not from mathematicians, but rather from the last place one would expect: the textile industry.

Textiles are phenomenally complex to manufacture. Thousands upon thousands of tiny threads must be woven together in precisely the right pattern, or else the cloth will be useless, or at least ugly to look at. When the complicated and demanding weaving process was handled solely by humans, the risk of mistakes was high; after long hours at a loom, a weaver was apt to misplace a thread and ruin the design of a fabric.

Ideally, this job should have been done by machines. A machine does not get tired and err from fatigue, and it would be much more reliable than human hands. But how could a mere machine be equipped to do the complex task of weaving?

Enter Joseph Jacquard. Where others in the textile industry saw only drudgery, he saw an opportunity to get rid of the error-prone human element in weaving, and to put the process on an automatic basis — thus saving time and money while improving the quality of the product.

Jacquard's idea was to build a weaving machine with a *program:* a set of instructions for weaving patterned cloth. The machine would and could do only what it was programmed to do. It would be totally reliable, and if programmed properly, would turn out cloth of uniformly high quality.

He devised an ingenious plan. The program would be cast in the form of punch cards similar to those enclosed in our telephone bills today. Jacquard strung the cards together to form an endless belt that passed over the hooks that did the actual weaving. Holes in the cards allowed the hooks to come up and snag threads of the warp, pulling them downward so that when the shuttle of the loom passed across, it would cross over some threads and under others, creating a pattern.

It was simple and nearly foolproof, and an immediate success. Jacquard introduced his loom in 1805 and, less than a decade later, saw more than ten thousand of them operating in France alone.

But the Jacquard loom had an impact far beyond the textile business. Across the Channel in England, a Briton named Charles Babbage took note of Jacquard's invention and was impressed by it. Though neither man knew it at the time, their inventions together would bring technology far along the road to the modern electronic computer.

Babbage was born in 1791, the child of a well-to-do Devonshire couple, and grew up to be one of the most famous inventors in English history. He was, as the British say, a bit odd. Babbage had a genius for abrasive behavior and turned practically every conversation into a dispute. (Charles Dickens reportedly used him as the model for the eccentric inventor Daniel Doyce, in *Little Dorrit*.) From time to time Babbage led crusades against elements of society that he found offensive, among them Italian street musicians. One such campaign ended in his being pelted with mud by an angry crowd. If his behavior did not inspire affection, then neither did his looks. His portraits show a man with a severe expression, cold eyes, a granite jaw, and a crooked slash of a mouth like the beak of a turtle. Babbage had the face of a man who would never admit he was wrong.

Despite everything, Babbage seems to have had a few friends. One of them was John Herschel, an astronomer and the son of William Herschel, discoverer of the planet Uranus. The younger Herschel once was working on some astronomical calculations with Babbage when the latter growled, "I wish to God these calculations had been executed by steam!"* Herschel replied, "It is quite possible." At that moment, Babbage was inspired to build a new kind of calculator.

This outburst sounds more like the genuine Babbage than the account he related in his memoirs. There Babbage said he conceived the idea of his calculating machine while poring "in a dreamy mood" over a book of logarithms. When a visitor asked what was on his mind, Babbage supposedly replied, "I am thinking that all these tables might be calculated by machinery." Most likely this story is just another of the romantic legends with which the history of science abounds, such as the tale of Newton and the falling apple.

However he got the idea, Babbage appears to have first thought of his calculating engine around 1812. Ten years later, in 1822, Babbage formally proposed building such a calculator, in a report to the president of the Royal Society, Sir Humphry Davy.†

Babbage's plan pleased Davy and the Society, who were all too familiar with the pain of doing long sums and products. Thus encouraged, Babbage did what any scientist in need of money would do today: he started looking for a government grant.

The Royal Society backed Babbage's scheme (even though Babbage himself was unsure how his machine might be constructed) and convinced the chancellor of the Exchequer that the project was worth funding. Babbage was on his way.

Babbage's "difference engine," as he called the machine, turned out to be a far more demanding project than he had ever expected, and in 1827 he worked himself into a nervous collapse. He took a holiday on the Continent to recover his health, and upon returning,

---

* When nineteenth-century scientists wanted to apply artificial power to something, they thought automatically of the steam engine, for gasoline and electric motors were still in the future.

† A pioneer in the chemistry of gases, Davy was also something like the psychedelic guru of his time. He made popular the breathing of nitrous oxide, or "laughing gas," as a recreation. This nineteenth-century high was thought to work by "concentrating ideas," the then current expression for mind expansion.

found that the government had renewed his grant. Refreshed, he went back to work with a will.

Progress was slow, however, and by 1842 the government's patience had run out. The prime minister and the chancellor of the Exchequer were alarmed at the cost of the project, and despaired of ever seeing any results from it. So they asked the Astronomer Royal, Sir George Airy, what he thought of the prospects for Babbage's engine. "Worthless," Airy told them, and the government dropped Babbage's plan like a hot stone.

But Babbage refused to quit. He continued working on his calculating machine, and, indeed, went far beyond his original plan. Soon he was thinking about a much more advanced calculator: something he dubbed the "analytical engine." It was to be a steam-powered machine with two principal parts: a "mill" to carry out arithmetical operations, and a "store" to manage the variables and the answers to calculations. To run the analytical engine, Babbage planned to use Jacquard's punch-card system. He would supply two sets of cards, one to tell the machine which operations to perform in which sequence, and the other to feed variables into the machine.

If this setup sounds familiar, it should, for Babbage had come up with the basic design for modern computers.

Computers in use today have three essential parts: a central processor to handle data and instructions fed into the machine; a memory unit; and a program to tell the machine what to do. Babbage's "mill" was the processing unit, his "store" was the memory, and his cards served as the program.

Unfortunately, Babbage never completed the analytical engine, for the steam-powered technology of his day was not up to the task. He died without realizing his goal of "calculating by steam." Eventually a small model of his machine was built, but only as an historical curiosity.

Shortly before Babbage died, the mathematician Lord Moulton visited him at his laboratory and later recorded his impressions of the old inventor and his still unfinished machine:

He took me through his workrooms. . . . There lay scattered bits of mechanism, but I saw no trace of any working machine. Very cautiously I approached the subject and received the dreaded answer, "It is not constructed yet, but I am working at it, and will take less time to construct it altogether than it would have taken to construct the Analytical Machine from the stage in which I left it."

Moulton called this visit to the pathetic old inventor "one of the sad memories of my life."

Other Britons had the same dream as Babbage. The physicist Lord Kelvin, who is best known for devising a temperature scale that has proven highly useful to science, wished somehow to construct a machine that would substitute "brass for brain" in calculating.*

But the British were about to give up their lead in technology to their former colony across the Atlantic Ocean. The Americans, not the British, would now take up where Babbage had left off.

Unwittingly, the Founding Fathers had done something that supplied an impetus toward the growth of computer technology. They had mandated, in the U.S. Constitution, that a national census be carried out every ten years. Originally the census was merely a matter of counting heads, but the immigrations of the nineteenth century made it advisable to keep track of other parameters as well: national origin, sex, number of children, et cetera. This task was so far beyond the information-handling capabilities of the mid-1800s that the census of 1880 was still unfinished by 1890. Desperate for some way to keep up with the flood of figures, Uncle Sam offered a prize to anyone who could invent an adequate data-sorting system.

Someone did. His name was Herman Hollerith, and he adapted the Jacquard punch-card system to the task of recording census data. The result was a great improvement in data-handling capability.

Hollerith invented a special keypuncher for entering data on the cards. It looked much like a telegraph key. Once punched, the cards passed through an electronic tabulating machine. An array of metal pins pressed gently against each card as it went by; wherever there was a hole in the card, a pin touched a conductor on the other side of

---

* Kelvin was known for his blunt wit. Once his students came to class and found a note on the door: "The Professor will not meet his classes today." As a joke, the students crossed out the "c" in "classes." Later they returned to find that Kelvin had crossed out the "l" as well.

the card, completing an electrical circuit and sending an impulse to a counting device. Hollerith's machines were installed in time to process the 1890 census, and performed so well that Hollerith founded a company to manufacture them. That company grew to be IBM.

But the Hollerith machine was still too slow for scientists. For that matter, so were the next few generations of information processors. Countless important problems in science were piling up because there was no way to solve them without a very rapid calculator. Would the right machine *never* come along?

Instead of merely wishing for a supercalculator, the Massachusetts Institute of Technology (MIT) faculty did something about it. In 1927, several members of the electrical engineering department completed work on an electronic machine that could work out simple differential equations.

Among the men responsible for this triumph was Vannevar Bush. A tall, gangling man with bushy hair and the manner of a benevolent stork, Bush was not satisfied with the performance of his first machine. Its capabilities were still too limited. What Bush wanted was a computer that could cope with more complex differential equations, of the kind that play in important role in engineering.

So Bush and his colleagues went back to work, and success was soon in coming. By 1931, they had invented a more advanced machine called the "differential analyzer." Unlike its predecessor, this device was totally mechanical, carrying out calculations by means of rotating shafts. The rotations stood for numbers and arithmetical operations.

The differential analyzer looked bizarre; somewhat like a giant dishpan full of parallel steel rods. Here and there gears turned, making the whole assemblage look like something from a Flash Gordon comic; one almost expected to see the Emperor Ming standing behind it and fingering his mustache.

Regardless, Bush's computer was successful. It was a good example of an "analog" computer, in which something substitutes for numbers and functions. The substitute may be the rotation of a shaft or disc, a change in the voltage of an electrical current, or whatever. The mileage indicator on an automobile is a very simple analog computer in which the rotation of numbered drums stands for distance traveled.

Quite different is the "digital" computer, which represents numbers just as on a written page — as a set of decimal or binary digits.

Here a word of explanation about number systems is in order. The decimal system is a "base-10" system: 0, 1, 2, 3, 4, 5, 6, 7, 8, 9. Some digital computers use it, but more often they utilize the binary "base-2" system. Binary arithmetic is what you would use if you could count on only two fingers. Translating from decimal to binary, we get:

0 = 0
1 = 1
2 = 10
3 = 11
4 = 100
5 = 101

And so on. Binary arithmetic is handy for electronic computers because it can be carried out easily with on-off pulses of electricity. A pulse of current stands for 1, an absence of current for 0. If computers were superstitious, they might be wary of Friday the 1101th and expect 111 years' bad luck after breaking a mirror.

Later in the 1930s, after Bush built his machine at MIT, Howard Aiken, a few blocks up Massachusetts Avenue at Harvard, was thinking about electronic computers operated by on-off electrical signals. In 1938, he began working with IBM to build a machine of that kind. Instead of using gears and whirling shafts to stand for numbers, the Harvard-IBM machine — called the Automatic Sequence-Controlled Calculator, or Mark I for short — utilized electrically operated relay switches.

At last Babbage's dream had come true. The Mark I was, in principle, the same machine Babbage had envisioned more than a century earlier. The technology of his day had simply not been equal to the task of building an automatic calculator. But where steam had failed, electricity worked. The Mark I was successful, even though it was as big as a PT boat and chirped like twelve exaltations of larks when operating. And it was dozens of times faster than the best human mathematician.

But that still was not fast enough. Though the Mark I could solve problems faster than "twenty Einsteins," as one newspaper article about the machine reported, engineers were soon looking for ways to shave time off the Mark I's performance.

The solution was to find a new kind of switch. The Mark I used switches opened and shut by electricity. Each switch took a good fraction of a second to open and close. Why not find a different kind of switch to do the job faster?

That needed component was the vacuum tube. It could switch on or off much more rapidly than a mechanical relay could. For that reason, vacuum tubes seemed the best bet for the next generation of computers.

The parent of that generation started taking shape during World War II at the University of Pennsylvania. With Army backing, the university began work on a vacuum-tube computer dubbed the Electronic Numerical Integrator and Calculator, or ENIAC.

Some engineers had misgivings about ENIAC. It was supposed to contain some 18,000 tubes, and even one or two burnouts might shut down the system. Just how reliable would such a fizzle-prone computer be?

But ENIAC foxed its critics and showed itself to be a highly dependable machine. Tubes usually cooperated, and ENIAC, a towering array of wire- and tube-filled cabinets that would have filled a fair-sized ballroom, often ran for a day or longer before a tube expired and forced the machine to stop. ENIAC handled many computing jobs during its lifetime (it was dismantled, though still in good working order, in the 1950s), among them calculations describing nuclear fission — the process behind the atomic bomb.

If the progress of computer technology, from the early machines of Pascal and Schickard up to ENIAC, seems to follow a familiar pattern, it should. Computers have been advancing (or evolving, if one wishes to stretch the meaning of the word slightly) along La-

marckian lines. When the Darwinists turned Lamarck's ideas into a
caricature of what he really said, Darwin's defenders were unwittingly building a model of *computer* evolution. Each generation of
computers is picking up a load of acquired traits — better circuitry,
to take one example — and passing those traits along to its descendants. Of course, the computers don't do so consciously (at least not
yet), nor are they self-reproducing organisms (though some highly
advanced computers do seem, at times, to come startlingly close to
the borders of living existence — a subject we will explore a bit
later). But otherwise, the pseudo-Lamarckian model of evolution fits
computer technology nicely. And this development marks a turning
point in the history of our species.

Up until now, our minds and bodies have been evolving in the
Darwinian mold: a long, slow process, full of chance events, and not
very systematic. It takes a long time for variations to occur naturally
in a species, and still longer to see how the variations work out, for
better or worse. But now a part of us — the electronic computer, the
"annex" that we created for our minds — is evolving in a much
faster and less haphazard mode, increasing our mental abilities all
the time.

Here we are assuming, of course, that the evolution of computers
is part of our own evolution as animals. Not all biologists and anthro-
pologists (or computer scientists) would agree with this judgment.
After all, one can argue that the evolution of a *tool* is not the same
thing as the evolution of a *tool-using animal,* for the same reason
that a mallet is not a man.

But at the same time, scientists are willing, even eager, to shout
"Evolution at work!" when some lower branch of the primate clan is
seen using tools, as in the already mentioned case of the chimp
breaking off a twig from a tree and using the twig as a probe or lever
to get at edible insect larvae. If a chimp showed up tomorrow waving
a stone-headed hammer he had made himself, nearly the whole scientific community would accept the evolution of the chimp's new tool
as a sign that the chimp was evolving, too.

So why should we deny that computer technology is part of *our*
species' evolution? There is no good reason to do so. The computers

have become part of our brains and minds, almost as much as our frontal lobes. Indeed, we are now so dependent on these extensions of our minds that we might perish without them, as surely as if some- one shot off the fronts of our skulls. Computers are now an integral part of us — as a society and as a species, if not always as individu- als. And as computers evolve more and more quickly, we can expect to see changes, in computers and in humankind, that will rival the de- velopment of the cerebral cortex in importance. That prospect is, in large measure, the work of one man, a Hungarian immigrant whose own, unassisted intellect was so powerful that he was rumored to be a Martian living incognito on earth. In a few short years he carried computer science — and therefore the extension of the human mind — as far ahead as it had progressed in the previous three cen- turies. We live, and will live for a long while to come, in a world he helped to make.

"More Important Than Bombs" | 6

Just before noon on August 6, 1945, the people of Hiroshima, Japan, were going about the normal activities of a summer morning when a faint droning noise overhead made them look up. They saw a U.S. B-29 bomber lumbering along in the sky: not an unusual sight, for the Americans flew over Japan almost unchallenged now, the Japanese air force having been swept from the skies. Sometimes the American planes arrived in great waves, bearing tons of high explosive to flatten cities and military targets. But this was a sole bomber, most likely on a reconnaissance mission — or so those on the ground thought.

When directly over the heart of the city, the bomber dropped something from its bomb bay. A cylindrical object fell out, deployed a parachute, and then drifted gently down over Hiroshima like a falling flower petal.

Inside the cylinder were several hundred pounds of uranium 235, divided into two chunks positioned at opposite ends of the bomb. On radio command, explosive charges inside the bomb would go off and slam the pieces of unstable uranium into each other, creating "critical mass" — the nuclear engineers' expression for an atomic explosion.

The signal went out, the explosives went off, the uranium chunks struck each other. And within a hundredth of a second the sky over Hiroshima exploded in nuclear fire.

How many persons died that day at Hiroshima, no one is certain, but most estimates range between 100,000 and 200,000. These figures include persons killed instantaneously by the heat and blast, and others who perished later from their wounds. Thousands more died still later from the lingering aftereffects of the explosion, such as cancer induced by radiation from the bomb, or birth defects in fetuses whose mothers suffered irradiation by the fireball.

The shock waves from the A-bomb blast over Hiroshima were political and social as well as physical. It is safe to say that except for the wheel, the lever, and the plow, no invention has done more to change the world than the nuclear bomb has. Two atomic explosions, both of them tiny by present standards, brought the long war in the Pacific to an end within days (the second bomb exploded over Nagasaki a few days after the Hiroshima attack). Since then, the foreign policies of the world's nuclear powers have been formulated mainly to prevent, if at all possible, the use of such weapons. And even so, the mere existence of nuclear bombs has brought the world to the edge of annihilation at least once, during the Cuban missile crisis of 1962.

Their existence has had odd effects on the human mind. Living under the constant threat of nuclear destruction, a whole generation has grown up accustomed to the idea that the world and everything in it might be destroyed one day in the space of a few hours. This knowledge has given us a curious indifference to mass slaughter; it is nothing uncommon these days to hear someone talk about "megadeaths" — each megadeath a million persons killed in a nuclear attack — as casually as if mentioning a dozen eggs in the refrigerator. Nuclear weapons have, at the same time, encouraged the growth of an "apocalypse mentality" in many of the developed nations; the threat of nuclear Armageddon is so close to Biblical visions of Judgment Day that one can hardly blame conservative Christians for thinking that the end of the world is nigh. Nuclear weapons undoubtedly are one reason why Americans are running to the churches in record numbers these days, trying to fend off their fears with prayer. And it all started with Hiroshima.

So it is interesting to hear what one of the bomb's creators, John von Neumann, had to say about it.

Von Neumann was one of the world's greatest mathematicians, and quite possibly the most brilliant one of all time. He was approached one day after World War II by a friend and colleague, Gleb Wathagin, who had spent the war years in South America. The physicist Freeman Dyson, in his memoir, *Disturbing the Universe*, recounts what happened at that meeting:

"Hello, Johnny," Wathagin said to von Neumann. "I suppose you are not interested in mathematics any more. I hear you are now thinking about nothing but bombs."

"That is quite wrong," answered von Neumann. "I am thinking about something much more important than bombs. I am thinking about computers."

Von Neumann was right. From an evolutionary standpoint, computers have turned out to be far more important than bombs. The nuclear bomb, for all its power, is merely another weapon. Though it has put some new fears into our heads, we were as a species — that is, as animals and especially as *intelligent* animals — about the same after Hiroshima as we were before it. Our mental capabilities were unchanged by the Bomb and its descendants. We seemed a bit more fretful but were still the same old minds in the same old bodies.

But the computer has changed all that. It has extended our minds in many ways. With computers, we can think faster and more comprehensively than ever before, juggling ideas that, before the computer age, were all but impossible for the unaided human mind to grasp, just as the mechanical extensions of our bodies, from automobiles to spacecraft, have made it possible for us to go places and do things that are impossible for our unassisted bodies.

We have seen the effects of this advance in mindpower all around us for the last few decades. Humans with computers at their disposal have great advantages over those who lack them. The computer-assisted physician, for example, has much more useful mental input than his or her computerless colleagues. Let us imagine, for example, that the doctor sees a patient who is complaining of severe shortness of breath. Any number of possible diagnoses come into the doctor's mind. Weak heart? Emphysema? Bronchitis? Tuberculosis? Each of these conditions would require a different treatment — and an error in diagnosis might prove to be highly embarrassing to the doctor, highly expensive to the patient, and perhaps even fatal. Physicians are all too keenly aware of the saying that "Doctors bury their mistakes."

So the M.D. calls on a computer for help. The computer is tied to a machine that measures the parameters of human breathing — lung capacity, amount of breath expelled in the first second, et cetera. When the patient exhales into a tube connected to that machine, data on the patient's breathing is gathered automatically and fed to the computer for analysis. The computer compares the data to a set of reference statistics that indicate how this patient's lungs ought to be performing at his age.

No doubt about it: this one has a lung problem. Lung capacity is only about 80 percent of what it should be. Even more significant is the fact that his FEV_1 — the computer's expression for the amount of air exhaled in the first second — is phenomenally low: only 30 percent of normal. That low value tells the computer that something is obstructing the patient's breathing. So the computer prints out on a tape: SERIOUS OBSTRUCTION IN BREATHING.

After checking out the patient by more conventional means — stethoscope, thermometer, blood pressure measurements, and so on — the doctor feels confident that the patient has a bad case of bronchitis. "I'm giving you an antibiotic and an inhaler," he tells the patient. A few days later, the patient is back to normal health, and the doctor chalks up another small victory for computer-assisted diagnosis.

This is, of course, just a minor example of how computers have extended our minds and improved our decision-making powers. In the world of business, multimillion-dollar judgments are made on the basis of computer projections. What will happen to auto sales in Virginia, for example, if the cost of gasoline rises two cents per gallon? Computer projections can provide a fairly good idea. Working on past data concerning auto sales, gas prices, and a few other related variables, the computer figures how many autos are likely to be sold in a given period just ahead, and even qualifies its own prediction with a percentage "confidence estimate": that is, there's a 90 percent chance that the actual sales figure will fall in between figure A and figure B. It would take human analysts quite a long time to perform this kind of analysis; the computer takes only a few minutes, and does it without error, provided that the data given it were accurate. This is what computer-extended minds can do.

Just as the Cro-Magnons were able to outwit the Neanderthals and beat them in the fight for survival, thanks to an extra bit of tissue in the frontal lobes of the Cro-Magnon brain, so the computer-aided human has a crucial edge over his or her computerless competitors. That, in essence, is what von Neumann meant when he said computers were more important than bombs. A bomb does nothing to augment anyone's intelligence.

Von Neumann's story begins in Budapest, Hungary, in 1903. He displayed his gift for math at an early age, and anecdotes of von Neumann's childhood resemble those told about Pascal. Once von Neumann's mother paused in the middle of her knitting and gazed pensively out into space. Her son noticed her abstracted look and asked, "What are you calculating?"

John von Neumann showed a phenomenal talent for figuring without the need for pencil and paper, and in later life his gift for working staggeringly complex math problems in his head was the wonder and dismay of his colleagues. Once a fellow mathematician decided to play a trick on him, and sat up all night working out the answer to a fiendishly difficult calculation. Next day he put the problem to von Neumann and asked for an answer. Von Neumann leaned back in his chair and stared at the ceiling for several minutes. Just as he arrived at the answer, his colleague announced it triumphantly before von Neumann could get a word out. Von Neumann was astonished and more than a little upset; he prided himself on his reputation as the fastest brain in mathematics, and didn't like to think that someone might be faster on the draw than he was. Fortunately for von Neumann's self-esteem, he was told how the prank had been set up.

Von Neumann viewed life in general as a set of equations to be solved. If he did not have the proper equation on hand for a given job, he formulated his own; and in so doing, he opened dozens of new vistas for math and for nearly all the other sciences as well. His daring and ingenuity brought him fame, wealth, and power, and his creations changed the world irrevocably.

Much of von Neumann's success may be traced to the social and political milieu of his homeland. As a scion of an upper-class Jewish family in a nation where anti-Semitism became official policy from time to time, John von Neumann felt with peculiar urgency the maxim, "Adapt or die." As his biographers have pointed out, this awareness seems to have made von Neumann, and many others in his generation of Hungarian intellectuals, think that survival depended on being brilliant and innovative. To avoid destruction, he had to come up with more and better ideas than anyone else. And as a rule, he *did* come up with more and better ideas than anyone else, and they gave him the prestige and material comfort he craved.

Von Neumann's career in school was predictably outstanding, and he did graduate work at Göttingen, the German Mecca of mathematical research. Here the mathematician Karl Friedrich Gauss, the Einstein of his day, had studied the orbit of the asteriod Ceres a hundred years earlier, and sketched the outlines of what would become non-Euclidian geometry.

At Göttingen, von Neumann and other young mathematicians, inspired by its traditions, took on an even greater task. They wanted not only to expand the scope of math, but also to firm up its whole existing structure.

In the previous few years, the foundations of math had begun to look shaky. The weak spots had turned up in a branch of mathematics called set theory, which deals with categories of things and how those categories may overlap.

The trouble with set theory was that it *looked* self-consistent, but on close examination it was seen to have some serious internal contradictions. Math must, of course, be self-consistent if it is to serve a useful purpose; two and two must always equal four, or else calculations will be in trouble.

So the flaws in set theory posed a big potential problem for mathematicians. If set theory had cracks in it, then who could tell what fatal inconsistencies might lurk in other fields of math? The mathematicians at Göttingen were in about the same position as a farmer who goes out to his cornfield one day and discovers a single ear of corn full of worms. If one ear is infested, then maybe the whole field is.

Von Neumann felt it was high time to put all of math on a solid footing. He had a vision of a thoroughly cleansed and purified science of mathematics where every proposition, every lemma, every last equation stood rock-bottomed and metal-sheathed, inviolable and provable, now and forever.

But von Neumann never realized that grand design. The spoiler in this case was a mathematician named Kurt Gödel.

Gödel demonstrated, in a famous proof that bears his name, that some propositions in math are beyond proving right or wrong. He showed that there are limits to the powers of logic and math, so that the dream of a science of math justified totally by logic — in short, what von Neumann had hoped to achieve — would always be merely a vision.

That dream shattered, the mathematicians at Göttingen turned their attention to other interests. One of von Neumann's was games: not the team kind (he was never inclined toward sports, and displayed a fine contempt for all athletics), but intellectual games such as checkers, chess, and cards. Here he was following the great tradition of Pascal and Fermat, and von Neumann's fascination with games would yield, long after his days at Göttingen, a new branch of mathematics every bit as important to the modern world as the two Frenchmen's work on probability.

Von Neumann's creation was game theory. Every game, whether played on a board or in a boardroom, follows certain rules of gain and loss. The rules are not always explicit, but all the same, they govern play just as effectively as the laws of physics govern the behavior of atoms. Game theory is far too complex to explain entirely in a few paragraphs, but a good qualitative example is the balance of nuclear terror between East and West. In this simplified case we will assume there are only two players, the United States and the Soviet Union. Now let us look at the relationship from the viewpoint of the Soviet leaders.

The goal of the game for the Soviets is to advance the interests of the U.S.S.R. all over the world, politically and militarily. To do this the Soviets must counter the influence of the United States. The Russians have several options:

1. *Peaceful coexistence.* This is undoubtedly the safest course: simply sit back and leave the rest of the world alone, trusting that everyone will flock to the banner of Soviet Communism. Unfortunately, this approach stands very little chance of success. Only one country in the past forty years has chosen a communist government in a free and open election; and wherever communists have taken over, large numbers of the population have voted with their feet in favor of other forms of government. So the Soviets had better try another approach.

2. *All-out war.* A nuclear attack on the United States would eliminate the competition from the game. On the other hand, the risk to Russia would outweigh any possible benefits, since the Americans, if attacked, would surely retaliate in kind, shooting off their missiles from underground silos and from submarines on patrol. Thermonuclear death would then descend on the Soviet Union as well as on the United States. That possibility is too awful to contemplate seriously, especially in the U.S.S.R., where memories of the last world war are still vivid. So pushing the button is impractical. What option is left?

3. *Something in between.* The best plan falls between these two extremes: more than peaceful inaction but less than total war. Try to wear the imperialists down. Engage them in lesser struggles all around the world, in little countries like Vietnam, so as to strain U.S. resources while generating domestic turmoil in America. At the same time, use spies and other covert operatives to subvert the United States from within, by stealing its secrets and recruiting other spies from among the native population. These efforts will bring the Kremlin some gains (not the total and sudden demise of the enemy, but still a gradual attrition of U.S. strength) while keeping the risk of Armageddon low. Ideally, this approach ought to net the Soviets an

optimum balance between risk and reward. Von Neumann called that situation a "minimax," or "saddle point." We and the Soviets have been seeking the best saddle point for years, in much the same manner as two calm, levelheaded poker players — each trying to maximize winnings while minimizing losses.

In this way, game theory has done much to shape our modern world. But game theory has its limitations, among them its own stress on rationality.

Von Neumann, in his formulation, took for granted that the players involved in a zero-sum two-party game, like the Cold War, would always act rationally and in their own best interest. So far that has been the case, at least as far as the United States and Russia are concerned.

But international politics is not always a rational game. Indeed, it can be quite devoid of logic and common sense. The Iranian revolution is a good case in point. Khomeini's revolutionaries acted in ways that violated every rule of self-interested thinking, and in their zeal, committed acts that harmed Iran more than America, the "great Satan" that the revolutionaries were sworn to destroy. This is one instance where game theory was useless for analysis. History is full of other examples; China's Cultural Revolution of the 1960s was the antithesis of rationality. And what would happen to a computer that tried to describe Caligula's reign in terms of game theory? Most likely the machine would reach the point where Caligula tried to make his horse a proconsul, and burn out a few circuits in astonishment.

So game theory doesn't always work. Indeed, its utility is limited to situations where all players are just as rational and self-interested as the Pentagon and Kremlin bosses. And even then, there are plenty of games in which it is hard to get the kind of neat, quantifiable result that appears, for example, at the end of a poker game.

Regardless, game theory has proven to be a powerful tool of math and of social analysis, and the mind that could conceive that theory would have been a tremendous asset to European science. Until the 1930s, it looked as if von Neumann would remain an ornament of Europe; he was comfortable in the German scientific community, spoke German fluently, and had the kind of genius Germany needed.

But Hitler had unpleasant plans for Jewish scientists such as von Neumann, who joined the mass exodus of European brainpower to America. Von Neumann ultimately settled at Princeton University, where he delighted the university community with his personal charm and engaging conversation (he was a master storyteller and had a vast repertory of jokes), while dazzling his fellow scientists with his mental power and versatility.

Von Neumann quickly became a Princeton legend. His parties and dinners were sumptuous, and invitations to them were as coveted in many circles as those from the White House. He was equally well known for his collection of dirty limericks, and nothing pleased him more than a ribald new addition to it.

Von Neumann was an unskilled driver, to put it mildly. He drove on either side of the highway with equal aplomb and wrecked cars on a regular basis. Once he even described one of his accidents in terms of relativity theory. "The trees on my right were passing in orderly fashion at fifty miles per hour," he said. "Suddenly, one of them stepped out in my path!"

One of von Neumann's prime traits, other than reckless driving, was intellectual restlessness. He was always on the hunt for new domains of knowledge to be conquered, especially if they happened to fall within his province — higher math. And in the early 1940s, he found a discipline of physics that would allow him to indulge his love for advanced math.

The discipline was hydrodynamics. Basically, hydrodynamics is the study of fluid motion. It is important to ship designers, who have to minimize the friction between a ship's hull and the surrounding water; hydrodynamics was also important to the engineers designing the first atomic bombs.

The bombs posed a special problem. The nuclear explosive inside them had to be set off by high-explosive charges, which were themselves tricky things to detonate. The high explosive had to be touched off in a certain way, or the bomb would be worthless.

In the first A-bomb, "Little Boy," the job was relatively simple. It was a "gun-type" bomb in which two chunks of uranium merely had to be clapped together, and boom: the instability of the uranium did the rest. There was no need for a very sophisticated high-explosive system to touch off the uranium charges.

The second A-bomb, "Fat Man" (named after Winston Churchill), was another matter entirely. Rather than a simple gun-type bomb, it was an "implosion" bomb. The nuclear explosive was arranged in a sphere at the heart of the bomb. To detonate it, conventional high-explosive charges would have to be set off all around the radioactive material, squeezing it inward just enough to generate critical mass. The problem was how to time the explosions precisely enough to make the bomb work. Even a slight error in synchronization would make the bomb a dud. If one of the charges fired an instant too late, then there would be a weak spot, or "asymmetry," in the explosion, and the main force of the nuclear blast would shoot off in the direction of the asymmetry, spoiling the effect of the bomb — in the same way that a hole in the side causes troubles for a water tank.

This problem delighted von Neumann. He saw that it would have to be tackled in two stages. One was to build a special high-explosive charge designed to send its blast inward evenly, with no asymmetries. The result was an odd-looking chunk of explosive shaped somewhat like the female breast. When detonated, the charge sent its explosive force inward, in the direction of the "breast's" flat side.

But von Neumann's second contribution was much more important. He showed the Los Alamos bomb team how to make mathematical models of the violent phenomena they were trying to control, and how to plug numbers into those models in order to get numerical answers. In short, von Neumann put the bomb on a firm mathematical foundation, just as he did the theory of games.

Some scientists would have had reservations about this kind of labor. After all, the Los Alamos group was trying to construct the most awesome weapon the world had ever seen — a bomb capable of wiping out entire cities with a single blast, taking innocent civilians along with any military targets in the vicinity, in a huge and undiscriminating fireball.

But von Neumann apparently had no qualms about his work. Its moral aspects did not enter into his calculations. He was ready to follow science and technology wherever they might lead, regardless of the consequences. Frankenstein, in Mary Shelley's novel, had much the same attitude, and in the end it destroyed him; apparently the same thing happened to von Neumann, as we will see shortly.

Von Neumann became a bomb aficionado. He attended postwar tests in the Southwest and seemed to delight in the spectacle of the great yellow fireballs rising over the desert. The explosions were an expression of raw power, and consequently a delight to von Neumann, who relished power and its exercise. His childhood experiences in Hungary had taught him that only the strong survive, and he made every effort to place himself among the strong. Other scientists made friends among philosophers, artists, clergymen. Von Neumann's friends were admirals, generals, and high-ranking civilian defense officials. He saw them as knights defending the world against the sinister Soviet colossus. That attitude was not unusual for a Hungarian; distrust and fear of the bear next door, von Neumann once explained, were common in his native land.

Still, von Neumann was anything but a warmonger. He generally avoided fanatical attitudes of any kind, including political ones. Therefore, his company was pleasant, and nearly everyone found him congenial (although some persons, put off by his reputation for infallibility, referred to him sarcastically as "Saint Johnny"). Von Neumann could put even the most nervous visitor at ease with his warm and friendly greetings. Old World charm, New World faith in technocracy, and perhaps the most formidable mind on the planet: that, in brief, is probably as close as one can come to describing John von Neumann.

One day in the summer of 1944, as the American A-bomb was nearing completion, von Neumann was waiting in a train station and happened to meet a mathematician from Philadelphia, Herman Goldstine. At first, Goldstine felt intimidated by von Neumann, who had about the same standing among mathematicians that the oracle at the temple of Apollo had among the ancient Greeks. But von Neumann's easy manner made him relax, and soon the two men were talking about Goldstine's work. Goldstine revealed that he was working on a new kind of computing machine that could carry out more than three hundred calculations per second.

All at once, "the whole atmosphere of the conversation changed,"

Goldstine recalled later, "from one of relaxed good humor to one more like the oral examination for the doctor's degree in mathematics."

Von Neumann was fascinated. Here was the kind of calculating machine that mathematicians had desired for centuries.

The machine was ENIAC. Von Neumann was eager to see it, and ENIAC's creators gave him the grand tour. Another intellectual world to explore! Von Neumann at once became immersed in computer science, and very soon he was thinking beyond ENIAC, toward a more advanced machine, which would be called EDVAC, for Electronic Discrete Variable Computer. And almost as soon as EDVAC took shape in his mind, von Neumann was thinking of still more powerful computers. He began to revolutionize the infant science of computers, summarizing, synthesizing, analyzing, and putting computer science on a solid footing.

Soon he was ready to report on his work. In 1945 he produced a 101-page paper entitled *First Draft of a Report on the EDVAC.* It was a logical blueprint for building computers. Von Neumann did not concern himself overmuch with the actual hardware required, for that part of the computer would undoubtedly change in the future. Instead, he outlined the logical structure of how computers process information. This report is to computers roughly what *Gray's Anatomy* is to the human body. Every computer in the world operates on the principles laid down in von Neumann's report.

Von Neumann was enthusiastic about the prospects for computer development. Indeed, he wrote the *First Draft,* he explained, so as to "further the development of . . . high speed computers . . . as widely and as early as feasible."

As more and more advanced computers became available, naming them became a kind of game. One was named the JOHNNIAC in von Neumann's honor. Von Neumann himself had the opportunity to name another computer. He christened it the Mathematical Analyzer, Numerical Integrator and Calculator — MANIAC.

Von Neumann turned his knowledge of computers to weather forecasting. Von Neumann built a mathematical model of the atmosphere and plugged weather data into it to produce forecasts. Some of the early results were ludicrous, including forecasts of summer snows in the Deep South. But in time the models were refined, and today computer forecasts of weather are commonplace. Each night, when the weatherman predicts the weather for the next couple of days, he is doing something that John von Neumann made possible. What was once said of Caesar might just as well be said of von Neumann: *Si monumentum requiris, circumspice* — if you want to see his monument, look around you.

Among von Neumann's other work was something that he was almost afraid to allow to leak out to the general public. He had been thinking about how organisms reproduce. In the typical von Neumann manner, he assumed that every organism was an automaton, a mechanism that could have its operation described in terms of known physical laws and mathematics.

A human is an automaton. So is a cat or mouse or virus. All these are self-reproducing automata. Now what, wondered von Neumann, would be required to enable an automaton to turn out copies of itself?

Four components, he decided:

First, an automatic "factory" that gathers raw materials and, following instructions from some other component, processes these materials into the specified form.

Second, a "copier" that takes those written instructions and copies them.

Third, a "control unit" that is connected to the copier and the factory and governs their operation.

Fourth, a "master program" that tells the "factory" how to manufacture the whole assemblage.

Von Neumann knew his theory could be misinterpreted, and knowing as he did the sensational streak in the mass media, had no desire to see the press take his ideas and turn them into wild tales about machines giving birth to little whirring babies. So von Neumann studiously avoided reporters. To a colleague at MIT he wrote that he had been "quite virtuous and had no journalistic contacts whatever."

As it happened, his theory of the self-reproduction of automata was correct. It described perfectly the reproduction of living things. Deoxyribonucleic acid (DNA), the material that carries the genetic code in cells, is the "master program." The "factory" consists of the ribosomes, sites of protein synthesis, which give the cell its "bricks and mortar." The control units and copiers are certain enzymes and other molecules. When all four components work together properly, they operate in a way that ensures success for both the cell and the organism of which it is a part.

Von Neumann had looked at living things as machines and obtained a priceless insight into the workings of life. But what about the inverse of that view? If organisms could qualify as mechanisms, then could mechanisms rate as organisms? Specifically, could an electronic computer — the artificial extension of the human brain — go a step farther and actually *replicate* the functions of the living human brain? Could the computer house a mind?

Von Neumann doubted it could. The dissimilarities between the computer and the human brain were simply too great, in his view. So little was known about the workings of the brain that von Neumann saw no sense in assuming it to be just a highly complicated digital computer (a commonly drawn analogy then and now). Also, von Neumann knew that knowledge of the brain's operation would necessarily progress at a crawl, because available research methods in neurology were so crude. (Von Neumann once compared those methods to studying the function of a computer by dropping bricks on its circuitry and observing the results.)

Von Neumann might have had different thoughts about brains and computers had he lived a few years longer. By the 1970s a revolution in computer technology was making it possible to pack more and more computing power into tinier and tinier volumes, thus carrying computers ever closer to the specifications of the human brain.

But von Neumann missed seeing that development. One day in 1955 he fell and injured his shoulder. When he had the injury treated, he was told that he had bone cancer. The disease was advanced, and von Neumann could reasonably expect to live only a few more months.

Ironically, von Neumann's own work may have destroyed him. He attended numerous bomb tests, and they surely exposed him to higher than normal levels of radioactivity. And the wild cells ravaging his body were one problem that even his incredible mind could not solve. Von Neumann had conquered the mystery of self-reproducing automata; now cancer cells, self-reproducing automata that reproduced all too well, were killing him. One has to wonder if he ever saw his affliction in that light.

John von Neumann died at Walter Reed Hospital in Washington, D.C., on February 8, 1957. His colleagues eulogized him in many ways. One suggested that von Neumann's genius marked his mind as that of a species "superior to man." Another compared him to Prometheus, descending from heaven with the gift of fire — but an intellectual fire, rather than a physical one — for the benefit of humankind.

In fact, the Prometheus analogy made some sense. Von Neumann had left behind a tremendous legacy. Because of his work, the powers of the human mind were now greatly extended, thanks to the thinking aid and mental prosthesis that he had helped to provide — the electronic computer, with its capacious memory and lightning-fast relays. Biological evolution would have taken millions or even billions of years to accomplish that feat; von Neumann and his colleagues did it in a single human generation or less.

Thanks to the "supercortex" that the computer provided, human intelligence appeared to be on the verge of a quantum leap ahead. And soon after von Neumann's death, further advances in computer technology began to make some of his own achievements in this field look as archaic as the Neanderthal's club.

Less Is More | 7

The story is told of a Chinese emperor who, for his court's amusement, called in a scholar and asked him to devise a game that would represent battle on a tabletop scale. The savant went to work on the problem and soon had a model ready for the monarch. What he presented to the emperor was the game now known in the West as chess. It differed slightly from modern chess sets; there were a couple of additional pieces on the board, including an elephant. But the game delighted the emperor, and he asked the inventor what he wished as his reward.

"Put one grain of wheat on the first square of the board," he replied, "two grains on the second, four grains on the third, and continue thus to the last square. The total amount of grain will be all I desire."

The emperor chuckled. "Done," he said, and commanded that the grain be brought and counted. With each square the grains multiplied . . . and multiplied . . . and multiplied. In a short while the total number of grains had reached a staggering level. One member of the court, astonished at how the progression had worked, turned to the emperor and said, "There is not enough grain in all our granaries to pay this man!" The scholar never collected his grain; instead, he was charged with some vaguely specified crime against the state, led out of the emperor's presence, and beheaded in a courtyard of the palace.

The story of the scholar's wheat sounds familiar to many computer scientists today, for the computing power of machines has roughly doubled every two years since the first electronic computers were invented. The computers of the early 1950s, for example, could perform several thousand arithmetical operations per second, perhaps four or five times more than the home computers presently on sale commercially. Now the most advanced computers can perform something on the order of one hundred million operations every second — so that if a computer started counting all the stars in our Milky Way galaxy, one by one, starting at the rim and working inward, the list would be done in a couple of hours. These computers are used, of course, for work considerably more important than counting stars; in fact, they are so rare that only thirty or forty computers with such capabilities exist in the entire world.

The post–World War II history of computers is a story of diminishing size and fantastically increased calculating power. As mentioned earlier, the first Bush-style computers were severely handicapped by their relay speeds. The relays were just too slow. It took a substantial slice of a second for a relay to open or shut, and so engineers once again faced the same problem that Leibniz and Pascal confronted centuries earlier — how to speed up the calculations.

Simple. Make the relays nonmechanical. Find some kind of switch or "gateway" that would open and close without the need to flip or twirl something. At first engineers decided the answer was the vacuum tube. It had no moving parts, and the improvement in performance was dramatic when vacuum tubes replaced mechanical elements. Mechanical relays took perhaps a tenth of a second to operate. A vacuum tube could do the same thing in less than a thousandth of a second and — better yet — was much less prone to breakdown. A vacuum-tube array roughly the size of an oatmeal box could add two and two in perhaps 0.0005 seconds. And although the tubes and all their associated wiring looked like a rat's nest constructed in a radio shop, the setup worked.

Yet the vacuum-tube models, for all their improvement over mechanical relays, were not fast enough for many uses. Even at a thousandth of a second per operation, many calculations could drag on for hours.

Also, vacuum tubes were bulky, and consequently, so were the machines that used them. Even a computer capable of merely working simple differential equations required a moving van to haul it, if the computer could be moved in one piece at all. And if someone had tried to duplicate only the functions of the human spinal cord (which are far simpler than most brain functions) using vacuum-tube technology, the result would have been a computer roughly as big as the Capitol building in the District of Columbia. At a conservative estimate, the computer would have contained enough wiring to reach from the earth to the moon.

Could the tubes be reduced in size? Better than that, engineers discovered, the tubes could be replaced entirely with a tiny new invention called the transistor. Made chiefly of the metal germanium, transistors acted much as the vacuum tubes did, but were smaller and much less prone to burnout, because they generated less heat. Transistors made possible a second generation of electronic computers that bulked smaller, ran cooler, and squeezed more computing power into less volume than anyone would have thought possible a few years before. The difference in sophistication between these first two generations of computers was roughly the same as between a fish's brain and a frog's. But whereas organisms took millions of years to carry out a change of this magnitude, computers did it in only a decade. This was Lamarckian evolution with a vengeance.

It looked as if transistorized units represented the smallest possible size for computer components. But not for long: the designers were still at work, and in the 1970s they created a new kind of "brain cell" for the computer — the silicon chip. Also known as the "integrated circuit," the chip is a wonder of miniaturization. It is also a work of art, in the same category with *La Gioconda* or Michelangelo's *David*. For beauty, sublimity, and compactness, it is hard to equal a chip. Enlarged diagrams of integrated circuits serve as wall decorations in computer science departments at colleges and universities all over the United States. A chip may look like a plumber's fantasia, or the Hampton Court maze, or one of Georges Braque's geometric layouts. Like the track of a snail far gone on LSD, pathways on the chip — the routes that electrons follow on their errands of arithmetic — fold back and forth across the tiny square of silicon, running parallel for a few thousandths of an inch, then making abrupt hairpin turns and running parallel again. The convolutions of the brain look simple compared to the patterns here. If the pathways on the chip were tubing, and one dropped a microscopic marble in the upper end of the tube, the marble would take about ten minutes to roll out the lower end. Don't stare at the diagrams too long; they can hurt the eyes after a minute or so. Stories are told of students who hypnotized themselves by looking overlong at a chip's blown-up image, then walked away in a dazed state and wandered into traffic.

Some chip designers sign their works as proudly as any professional portraitist does, and they react with the wounded pride of artists when they see their works stolen and copied by the Soviets, who will stop at nothing to match the West's current edge in chip technology. The Soviets copy the pilfered chips right down to the tiny fillips of layout that serve as the chip designers' signatures. "It's like seeing those $4.95 plaster copies of Rodin's *Thinker*," one designer told me with an embarrassed smile.

The fabrication of a chip is a long and exacting process. It begins with the growing of an ultrapure silicon crystal in a vat of molten silicon. A pure silicon crystal is inserted into the melt, and, atom by atom, much as sugar crystals grow in honey, the crystal accretes and grows, until it is perhaps the diameter of a grapefruit. Then the crystal is removed, cut into thin slices, and prepared to receive a circuit pattern.

Human designers and computers work together on the circuit design. The humans conceive the general pattern — "rough it out," one might say — and then hand it over to the precise and patient computer to have the edges smoothed. In this limited way, computers are taking part in their own reproduction: a potentially awesome development that we will discuss more thoroughly in a later chapter, for it may bear on our whole concept of life versus nonlife.

While the design is being prepared, the thin wafers of silicon sliced from the crystal are "cooked" in a special oven. In a carefully controlled oxygen atmosphere, the wafers react with the oxygen to form a thin layer of silicon dioxide over their surface. Silicon dioxide is the same compound that makes up ordinary window glass. It is transparent and has no effect on the wafers' appearance. They enter the oven looking like thin gray cookies and come out looking just the same.

But the glassy coating does affect the wafers in an important way. While silicon will conduct electricity, silicon dioxide will not. (That property makes glass perfect for use as electrical insulation on telephone poles.) So, with the help of a technique called "photolithography," technicians can turn the chip into a fantastically intricate tracery of conducting and nonconducting material.

Lithography has been around for more than two hundred years. Currier and Ives used it to preserve the images of nineteenth-century America, and Honoré Daumier used it to chronicle the human comedy of Paris. As used by artists, lithography is simple. The artist uses a greasy crayon to draw a design on a block of fine-grained limestone. Then a water-based ink is rolled across the stone. When a sheet of paper is pressed down on the inked stone, a reverse image of the picture on the stone is transferred to the paper. Hundreds of pictures can be made in this way from a single stone, before the original drawing fades and has to be redrawn.

Photolithography works on a slightly different principle. Here ultraviolet light, the same kind that gives you a suntan, replaces ink, and silicon chips replace the paper.

Rather than drawing a picture on the stone, the chip makers fabricate a "mask" with the circuit design imprinted on a transparent disc. The disc allows light to pass through, except in opaqued areas corresponding to the final desired pattern on the chip.

When ultraviolet light shines through the mask in a light-dark pattern, it alters the character of the wafer's surface. Areas exposed to the light are hardened, while unexposed areas are not. The softer spots can then be washed away by special chemical treatments, leaving on the chip's surface the desired pattern of conducting and nonconducting materials.

Of course, this is a highly simplified account of the process. In practice it is much more complicated and can be used to produce extremely complicated chips with multilayered structure. Under a microscope, some of these chips look like tiny shopping malls, or native American cliff dwellings, or a weirdly jumbled layer cake.

When the silicon wafer came out of the oven, it was a featureless gray disc. Now, after photolithography, it looks like plaid cloth, each check in the plaid a tiny, intricate circuit. With special cutting tools, the disc is partitioned into minuscule squares, each one bearing a circuit. A typical wafer yields about two hundred circuits of the "large-scale" variety, "large" in this case meaning roughly the size of a small pea. One by one the circuits are snapped off from the rest of the wafer, and each circuit is then tested on a special diagnostic machine to see if the circuitry works right. The testing machine looks like a sunflower built out of dental probes. The tips of the "probes" focus inward on the tiny chip, which nestles in the heart of the "flower" like a miniature honeybee while inspectors peer at it through a microscope, poking it with contact needles to see if everything functions properly. If faulty, the chip is discarded; if approvable, it may wind up in anything from a home computer to a talking doll.

Even this technology, which would have seemed sheerest fantasy in von Neumann's lifetime, is starting to look almost neolithic, as computers develop farther and farther each year. The circuitry of computers is now approaching the human brain in density, and very soon we may expect to see chips containing as many circuits as there are cells in an equivalent area of our cerebral cortex. Photolithography can etch fifty thousand to one hundred thousand circuits on a single pea-sized chip. In the near future that figure may stand closer to one million, thanks to new methods of "drawing" circuitry on chips with a "pencil" far more accurate than a light beam.

Down to a certain order of magnitude, light works fine. But below a scale of about one micron — a millionth of a centimeter, or approximately 0.0000004 inches — even light waves become huge and cumbersome. Each light wave used in the photolithography process has a wavelength of roughly half a micron to a micron. That is much too large to burn out micron-size features on a chip, which is what the chip makers want to do. Like the scholar in the chess story, they wish to keep packing stuff into a very limited space; and the more circuits they can fit on a chip, the better.

But if even light waves are too big to handle on this scale, what *will* do the job? Fortunately, there is something that gives even better resolution than a light wave: the electron.

Electrons are the negatively charged particles that swarm around the nucleus of an atom, forming the atom's outer shell. The electrons give atoms their chemical properties by darting in and out of the shell. Exactly what electrons really are, it is difficult to say; when things get this tiny, the lines between objects and energy and pure mathematics are hard to draw. Electrons are so little that they have virtually no mass at all — less than a thousandth the weight of the positively charged and neutral particles, protons and neutrons, in the nucleus. So tiny and insubstantial are electrons that physicists have almost quit thinking of them as particles, and now see them instead as stationary vibrations, or "standing waves," in the shells of energy that surround the nucleus. But the electrons can be made to behave as particles. They can be loaded into "guns" and fired like buckshot at a target. And so they can be used to draw patterns on chips, much as Sherlock Holmes used his revolver to write a patriotic "V. R." in bullet holes on the wall of his Baker Street flat.

Presently, physicists can fire a beam of electrons only a couple of atoms wide, and trace letters and numbers only a couple of microns high. With "e-beam lithography," as this new technique is called, one could copy out the *Encyclopaedia Britannica* on a pinhead and fit the entire contents of the Library of Congress onto a postcard or two. E-beam lithography is to photolithography as a sharp pencil is to a paint roller.

With such tools at their command, chip makers are starting to wonder just what the lower size limit on a chip may be. Now and then a computer specialist, slightly in his cups after a couple of beers (for computer experts, two drinks constitute a bender), will start speculating about the development of "supermicroprocessors," chips so tiny and so packed with circuitry that virtually every *atom* will have a specific job. In principle, it could be done. In practice, it probably won't, for there are constraints on the smallness of chips. One is cost. Shrinking a chip is an expensive process, beyond a certain point. An ultraminiature chip may cost tens of millions of dollars to design, and that expenditure is hard to justify if already existing chips, themselves almost too tiny to be seen with the unaided eye, can do the job as well.

Nonetheless, chip design is advancing fast. The chips may not get much smaller in the years ahead, but they will almost surely get "smarter." New materials may help, among them an exotic compound called gallium arsenide. A union of arsenic and gallium, a silvery metal with a very low melting point, gallium arsenide can do the job now performed in chips by silicon, but can do it much faster.

Electrons race through gallium arsenide roughly five times faster than they do through silicon, so a gallium arsenide chip could do calculations much more quickly than a silicon-based chip could. In a business where speed is of the essence, that saving in time could add up to a big saving in money; with a gallium arsenide chip inside, a computer could transmit data so fast that the cost of the computer time would fall dramatically. Here again, however, cost is a limiting factor. Gallium arsenide is expensive. A couple of ounces of it can cost as much as a suburban home; a pound, as much as a whole office building. Will the cost of gallium arsenide offset the savings from faster calculations? No one is rushing out to buy gallium arsenide futures until the computer industry sees just how cost-effective this new compound really is.

Fortunately, there are plenty of other ways to speed up calculations. One is the heatless junction, which neatly overcomes one of the biggest problems faced by computer designers today — heat buildup.

Looking at a minuscule chip, all but lost in the palm of your hand, it is hard to see how anything so small could put out enough heat to cause trouble. And an individual chip doesn't emit much heat at all. When innumerable chips are jammed together in a small space, however, and each chip holds hundreds of thousands or even millions of junctions, each one giving off a little warmth as it opens or shuts to control electron flow, heat can build up quickly, just as the little bits of grain accumulated fast on the scholar's chessboard. Soon the warmth can reach hazardous levels. It can damage components or even melt the chips. So the chips must be kept apart, and this packing problem means it is hard to shrink computers past a certain point. In a computer, as in a crowded room, closeness can make things too hot for comfort.

Yet computers must keep shrinking if they are to increase their speed. Every extra millimeter of wire or other circuitry is that much farther that electrons have to travel; and the longer the distance, the slower the calculation. To us there may not seem much difference in travel time between a wire one inch long and another one-hundredth of an inch long. But in the nanosecond world of the computer, where time has to be split as finely as possible, a *billionth* of a second can seem like an eternity. (That is about the time it takes a wave of light to cross the diameter of a hydrogen atom. To illustrate in another way, a billionth of a second is roughly equivalent to one second out of thirty-two years.)

This is where the heatless junctions come in. They give off so little heat that they can be packed in awe-inspiring densities. Cooled by a bath of liquid nitrogen, to soak up even the faint heat produced, a computer of the future may have all the capabilities of a whole building full of today's best computers — yet be no bigger than a watermelon.

The fastest computers today are awesome enough. Known generically as "supercomputers," there are only a tiny handful of them in the whole world, and they are reserved for the most fiendishly difficult calculations, of which there are plenty in science and engineering. Supercomputers can handle approximately one hundred million arithmetic operations in a second. (If you assigned a supercomputer to do a nose count of every last human being on earth, roughly four billion persons, the computer would say the equivalent of "all done" and present you with the total less than a minute later.)

Supercomputers owe their fantastic speed to a variety of new technologies and programming techniques. One of the latter is "vector processing," in which long ordered lists, or vectors, of data items are lined up side by side, so to speak, putting each operation on one list right next to a similar operation on the adjacent list. Then the computer can do both these "paired operations" at the same time.

Strange and wonderful things happen to data when a supercomputer is around. Here we see just how far electronic computers have extended the limited mathematical abilities of our own brains. Suppose — to take a whimsical example — you want a description of how airflow behaves around a thrown football. The halfback heaves the ball down the field in a long pass, and the ball slices through the air at perhaps thirty miles per hour.

The football doesn't simply part the air. It creates a complex pattern of eddies, discontinuities, shock waves, and other fluid-flow phenomena, with names almost as long as the football field. The roughness of the ball's surface creates weird effects. So does the slight corkscrew motion imparted to the ball by the twisting of the player's hand. How can one model this bewildering mass of swirls and curlicues accurately?

It's not easy. To describe the flow patterns with perfect accuracy, one would have to keep track of every last air molecule in the vicinity of the ball, and, of course, that is impossible. The best one can do is set up a three-dimensional grid of coordinates around the ball, an invisible scaffolding that exists only in the mind, and note the passage of selected bits of air with reference to that grid. Clearly, this involves a staggering amount of data. Even if you count only one in every million air molecules, the total information might fill a whole library and keep ordinary computers busy for months digesting it. But with a supercomputer, problems like this are relatively easy. The supercomputers could give you a reasonably accurate picture of the complex flow pattern around the football, from the moment it took flight until the instant it smacked into the receiver's hands. *This* is computing power.

The supercomputer's effects are not confined to numbers. Odd things also happen to the English language when supercomputers are around. People start talking about "megaflops" — each megaflop standing for a million "floating-point operations," or calculations involving scientific notation (say, 1.2×10^3 multiplied by 6.5×10^{10}).

Data operands. Pairwise operations. Pipelined scalar arithmetic. The few humans who inhabit the realm of the supercomputer speak in surreal vocabularies that conjure up bizarre images in the minds of laymen. Pipelined scalar arithmetic, for example, makes one think of someone counting huge reptiles crawling out of a culvert. And if a computer programmer walked onto the floor of a stock exchange and shouted, "Hey — there's been a phased bank partition," bankers might start jumping out of windows before he revealed it was a programming technique used to keep data flowing smoothly through the computers.

Marvelous as they seem, supercomputers are less than impressive when one finally sees them. Hollywood has given us a mental picture of some monstrous bank of flashing lights and twirling discs. The real thing is quite different. A supercomputer is more likely to look like a big cable drum or a bland piece of outdoor sculpture. The supercomputer installed at NASA's Ames Research Center, for example, resembles a giant stack of pineapple rings. About one and a half times the height of a grown man, it consists of a cylinder six feet wide, with a hole down the middle and about a dozen partitions radiating out from the center. A ring of padded benches surrounds the central tower; under the cushions is the computer's power supply. If you saw the machine in a suburban shopping mall, you might presume it was just an elaborate bench, and never suspect you were sitting on a magnificent extension of your own brain and mind.

Even the supercomputers may look primitive in a few more years. As mentioned previously, the speed and capabilities of computers have been doubling roughly every two years for the last two decades, and there seems every reason to think that trend will continue. Already computer designers are said to be thinking of ultracomputers capable of doing a billion arithmetical operations per second, and very possibly some visionaries are thinking beyond even *that*.

But for all their power and sophistication, supercomputers are still monumentally stupid. They are mammoth number-crunchers and not much more. They can tell you the point of impact of a marble dropped from the top of a skyscraper during a hurricane, but more complicated "thinking" is beyond them. They remind one of the brontosaurs: big and mighty and unexcelled at what they do, but not too bright. The little dinosaurs like *Stenonychosaurus* had better general-purpose information-processing systems in their heads, and those dinosaurs forged ahead on the scale of evolution, becoming more and more intelligent with each passing megayear. Their programming was improving along with their flesh-and-blood "computers." Had extinction not caught up with them, those dinosaurs would probably have gone on to evolve a humanlike intelligence.

Will the same happen to computers? Will they, under our guidance, evolve along Lamarckian lines into intelligent beings? Will we be able to extend our intelligence — whatever that may be — into machines, making them think like us and for us, in effect evolving whole extra brains and minds for ourselves?

Thomas Henry Huxley suspected we might, someday. He was persuaded that scientists would sooner or later arrive at a "mechanical equivalent of consciousness": a kind of thinking program that could be implanted in an artificial machine just as our thinking program, what we know as intelligence, is implanted in a natural machine. That prospect has beguiled and haunted the scientific community for years — notably one brilliant but highly eccentric scientist whose work helped to reshape our notion of what life and intellect really are.

"I Am a Machine" | 8

Down a long corridor at the Massachusetts Institute of Technology he waddled: a stout man with spectacles and bulbous eyes, a white goatee, and a peculiar ducklike walk. He looked every inch the image of the absentminded college professor. At the moment he was on his way to deliver a lecture in higher math, but he was unsure where the classroom was, and consequently he walked in on the wrong class without realizing it. Oblivious to his error, he started into his talk. But no one minded; Norbert Wiener's lectures were grand entertainment.

For more than thirty years, Wiener was the pride and joy of MIT, as well as one of the world's leading computer scientists and mathematicians. His labors helped pave the way for a new and better understanding of what intelligence is and how it works; and Wiener's concerns about the uses and possible abuses of intelligence (whether natural or man-made) led him to pose some disturbing questions that still trouble the scientific community.

Norbert Wiener was born in 1894, the first child of Leo and Bertha Wiener. Leo Wiener was a Harvard University faculty member and an immigrant from Russia. He had met Bertha while teaching in Missouri and had married her in 1893. Their son Norbert was destined for an agonizing childhood, for Leo wanted his child to be a genius, and put the boy through rigorous intellectual training at home. The results were spectacular: Norbert was reading at age three, and by age six was familiar with the writings of Charles Darwin. He was drilled relentlessly in math, and whenever Norbert made an error in his lessons, his father tongue-lashed him to the point of tears. But fortunately for Norbert, Leo Wiener had a softer side as well; he took his son on walks through the woods, identifying flora and fauna for him, and sometimes collecting specimens to take home. With his father, Norbert toured museums and factories, soaking up the wonders of science and technology. Leo also gave Norbert free run of the family's large and varied library, where the boy read about almost every conceivable subject. He learned still more from the distinguished intellectuals who visited the Wiener home. It was a grand place for a brilliant young mind to grow and flower.

Of Norbert's brilliance there was no question. When only eleven years old, he entered Tufts College (now Tufts University) in Medford, Massachusetts, just outside of Boston. Three years later he had his degree, and at age fourteen he started attending Harvard as a graduate student. What he gained in intellectual ability from his early training, however, was offset by the emotional scars left by his father's brutal regimen. Norbert knew how to work integrals and invert a matrix, but he had little comprehension of human feelings, his own or anyone else's. Norbert was both a mental athlete and an emotional cripple, full of painful memories and resentments that would plague him all the rest of his life.

Bertha Wiener compounded the emotional hurts to her son. Though she and her husband were of Jewish extraction, Bertha Wiener loathed Jews and communicated some of that prejudice to her son. She warned Norbert that Jews were greedy, lazy, and untrustworthy; and so, when Norbert finally learned of his Jewish ancestry, he was wounded more deeply than words could express. He looked into the mirror and saw the features of the hated Jew looking back at him; and he realized he was what he had been taught to despise. He never forgot that pain.

Norbert could hardly help feeling that his parents, in trying to give him what they considered a proper upbringing, had instead played a very dangerous game with him, in fact, had run the risk of destroying him. In his autobiography, *Ex-Prodigy*, he wrote a solemn warning for all parents who set out to make their offspring into *Wunderkinder:*

Let those who choose to carve a human soul to their own measure be sure that they have a worthy image after which to carve it, and let them know that the power of molding an emerging intellect is a power of death as well as a power of life.

Norbert felt all too keenly that he had been a deliberate creation of his father's intellect, a little thinking machine that could be programmed to think like a genius. Once Leo Wiener had written in a poem: "I am a machine. . . . How should a machine ever come to think?" In later years Norbert and other scientists would take up his father's notion of a thinking machine and use it as the basis for a whole new science.

After taking his doctorate in mathematics from Harvard, Norbert went on to Europe for postdoctoral study, and while there he did not endear himself to the leading mathematical minds of Europe. Bertrand Russell thought the young Wiener had been spoiled by too much flattery: "[He] thinks himself God Almighty," Russell complained in a letter to a colleague. Wiener also managed to antagonize the great David Hilbert. Much of Wiener's problem was mere insecurity: he was desperately worried about what others thought of him, and especially that they might consider him (as he confessed in a letter to his mother) "a fool." Therefore, he tried so hard to impress others with his brilliance that he wound up instead with the reputation of a bumptious, though gifted, boor.

But Uncle Sam wanted him, if no one else did, and in World War I, he worked as a mathematician for the army, at the Aberdeen Proving Ground in Maryland. A group photo of the mathematicians in his unit at Aberdeen, taken in 1918, shows Wiener standing at the far right, a plump, upright figure with round spectacles and a bushy dark mustache. He looks more like a grocer or butcher than a soldier and mathematician.

Shortly after the war Wiener was hired to teach math at MIT, thus beginning an association that would last the rest of his life and would benefit both Wiener and the Institute greatly. MIT was, around 1920, little more than just another engineering school. Its days of glory were still a decade or two in the future. But Wiener settled comfortably into his MIT job and started working on mathematical problems that had interested him for years.

His interests were not limited to pure math. Thanks partly to his father's guidance, Wiener had developed a taste for engineering and philosophy as well as mathematics. More importantly, he had developed a gift for synthesis, and could bring together elements of perhaps half a dozen different disciplines to form a grand design much greater and more useful than the sum of its parts.

Perhaps his most famous synthesis was cybernetics. It was based on a whole new way of looking at the universe and at the way all its multiverse components work. Take living things, for instance. What makes them operate? What keeps them going?

Traditionally, the answer was something like this: energy keeps them going. Solar energy reaches the earth and is converted into chemical energy through photosynthesis. Plants store that transformed energy in the form of carbohydrates and then pass it along to other organisms by a vast number of chemical and physical processes. But ultimately it all boils down to energy — or so scientists thought until Wiener came along. Wiener took a different view. Energy, he suggested, is less important to life than *information*.

Many of the everyday events and processes we see taking place around us, from the growth of corn to the birth of children, are as much exchanges of information as anything else. And so, once we understand how information — and which information — is transferred within a system, we can better understand how that system works.

Information transfer, communication — call it what you like — it provides (Wiener said) a handy unifying theme for many different kinds of scientific studies. Seen in terms of cybernetic theory, for example, humans and machines start looking very much alike.

Consider cars. A fuel-injection automobile does basically the same thing as a human body: it oxidizes fuel. For the human body, that fuel is carbohydrate, while the car burns hydrocarbons; the auto burns its fuel much more rapidly than the human body does; but these are minor differences. Both systems operate on the same fundamental principles.

In each case, the oxygen has to be delivered at a certain rate for best performance — not too fast, and not too slowly. Humans have evolved an elegant and highly efficient control mechanism for this job. Oxygen enters the body through the lungs and is absorbed into the bloodstream. At the same time, carbon dioxide, the waste product of respiration, is transferred from the blood into the lungs and exhaled.

The important thing is to strike the right balance between these two processes. If oxygen is coming in too slowly relative to carbon dioxide disposal, then carbon dioxide will start building up in the bloodstream, making the blood a bit too acid. (In this case the acid is carbonic acid, H_2CO_3, the product of carbon dioxide, CO_2, and water, H_2O.) When the acidity of the blood starts rising, a cluster of acid-sensitive cells in the brain registers the change and automatically signals the lungs to start pumping a little harder, so as to bring in more oxygen and lower the acid concentration in the blood.

Thus the body is guaranteed a steady supply of oxygen. The process is self-regulating: luckily for us, because if our conscious minds had to control it, then we might forget to breathe, and die of asphyxiation.

Much the same thing goes on in a fuel-injection car. To maintain just the right balance between fuel and oxygen in the engine, the car uses an electronic sensing system to monitor several variables (the kind of fuel being used, the oxygen concentration in the outside air, et cetera) and set the fuel/air ratio at the optimum value.

In humans and in cars, this regulating process is at bottom an information transfer. The brain, in effect, tells the lungs that more oxygen is needed, and the lungs respond. The car's fuel-injection system "decides" that more fuel or air is needed to get the best mileage per gallon, and the engine responds. And although a person and an automobile are two very different things, they operate on many of the same cybernetic principles. Each of us might then say, with Leo Wiener, "I am a machine" . . . at least up to a certain point. But where is that point? Where and when does a mechanism cease to be merely that, and become something more — say, an individual human being?

As Norbert Wiener demonstrated, the dividing line between mechanisms and organisms can be hard to draw. Von Neumann said as much in his theory of self-reproducing automata. And that fuzzy borderland between the living and inanimate, between the human and the machine, troubled Wiener greatly. He did not like to think of humans as machines, for it distressed him to imagine the human personality, in all its depth and richness and unpredictability, reduced to a set of equations and information transfers. Wiener was a humanist in the best sense of the word — a person who wished to see humankind freed from the shackles (political, psychological, or whatever) that impede its progress toward greater wisdom and happiness. He had a libertarian vision of what society ought to be: a place in which every person should have the chance to develop his or her potentialities to the fullest, with equal opportunity and justice for all, regardless of the individual's social station. Wiener longed for a society where no one would be allowed to "enforce a sharp bargain by duress" on anyone else. None of these goals was compatible with the idea of humans as machines. A machine is a *thing,* a tool, a lifeless object without rights or feelings; a human is quite a bit more than a machine. Wiener saw this distinction plainly; sad to say, not all scientists do, and the world is poorer for their blindness.

Just as he feared that humans might one day be reduced to the status of machines, Wiener worried also that machines might, as technology advanced, rise from the level of machinery to — what? Intelligence? Life? An intelligent machine might be life by definition, since all the intelligent beings we know are alive. And such a machine would be *a creation of humans.*

The idea of synthetic life and artificial intellect fascinated and haunted Wiener almost all his life. From childhood he was interested in the notion that one might animate lifeless matter by reciting the proper "incantation" over it. And with the advent of electronic computers, which transferred information more adeptly than any other devices humans had made, perhaps the incantation could at last be put into the right words, and inform the inanimate how to come alive.

There were plenty of precedents in legend. Wiener's favorite was that of the golem, a statue supposedly made and brought to life in sixteenth-century Prague by chief rabbi Judah Löw ben Bezalel. Worried about the persecution of his people, the rabbi decided that the Jews of Prague needed better intelligence about what was happening in the gentile camp: above all, when pogroms were about to occur.

But a spy's job was dangerous, and the rabbi hesitated to send a person when there might be a better way to glean the needed information. Why not, he mused, create an *artificial* spy? A daunting task, to be sure, but did not the holy book say that all things were possible with the help of God?

So one evening the rabbi took two companions out to the riverbank, and they collected enough clay for a man-sized figure. Soon a statue was ready, and the rabbi started the incantations that he hoped would bring his creation to life. A verse here, a chant there, and gradually the life-giving information was implanted in the clay form. Lastly, the rabbi inscribed the name of God on the statue's forehead, and the being came alive. It needed a name. The rabbi chose Joseph Golem.

Soon the golem was shuttling between the synagogue and the rest of Prague on spy missions for the rabbi. But it was hard to tell, on balance, whether the rabbi's marvelous creation was an asset or a liability, for there was a perverse streak in the golem's character, perhaps a result of the rabbi's having used low-grade clay. The golem liked to play practical jokes, one of which came close to flooding the rabbi's household. And on occasion the golem could become violent. Once, he assaulted the rabbi, who concluded that the experiment would have to be terminated, and erased God's name from the statue's forehead. Immediately the golem disintegrated into dust, and the rabbi had to look elsewhere for secret agents.

There are many variations on the golem legend, from the Sorcerer's Apprentice to Frankenstein's monster; and in nearly all these tales the ending is the same. The synthetic intelligence of the golem-figure turns out to be seriously flawed, and its creator learns that he cannot create a perfect, or even near-perfect, intelligence. The experiment is always doomed to disappointment, if not total failure — a lesson that some of Wiener's colleagues in computer science would learn by painful experience when they tried to extend parts of the human intellect into the circuits of computers.

Wiener saw parallels all too clearly between the golem legend and the biblical story of creation. In the Scriptures, God creates what he intends to be a perfect world, then is forced to sit by and watch it deteriorate, in the same sad manner as Rabbi Löw. And Wiener believed that if humans ever were able to create an artificial mind, thus arrogating to themselves the role of God, then they were likely to have no more success than the God of the Bible, or the rabbi. Humans, Wiener thought, were not yet ready to play gods; and if they ever were, then they would run the risk that any experiment in synthetic intelligence, if successful, might end in disaster for both creator and creation.

Wiener spent his last years roaming the halls at MIT, worrying about the risk of nuclear war, pondering some fresh idea or equation, and pausing occasionally to pop a peanut into his mouth. A cartoon of him, published in a student newspaper, shows him standing splay-footed outdoors, spherical head tilted back and mouth agape to catch a nut sailing upward from one plump hand. Sometimes he would stop in the hallways to chat with students, and while talking forget completely what business had brought him out in the first place. "Where was I going?" he would ask, hoping someone could enlighten him.

Wiener died of a heart attack in 1964, while on a trip to Europe. As he neared the end of his life, the prospect of building an actual golem, an artificial construct into which humans might extend not only their reasoning process but also their consciousness as well, was looking more plausible all the time — thanks in part to the work of a gifted young Englishman whose life ended all too soon.

"His Mind Was Disturbed" 9

The inquest ruled it a suicide.

One day in 1954 the body of a forty-one-year-old man was found at his home in England. A spoon coated with cyanide, possibly the product of an amateur chemistry lab he kept in his house, was found near the body. Officially, he was declared to have poisoned himself while "the balance of his mind was disturbed."

The suicide's name was Alan Turing, and in his short lifetime Turing did more than perhaps anyone else to expand our visions of what computers can do. Turing was one of Europe's leading experts in computer science, and one of its most gifted mathematicians as well; had he lived longer, there is no telling what marvels he might have achieved. Unfortunately, he ran afoul of his nation's religious superstitions, and a widespread moral prejudice appears to have led to his demise.

Turing was born in 1912. The son of an Indian Colonial Service employee, Turing grew up in England (although in a sense he never grew up, as we will see shortly). In school he had difficulty learning subjects that failed to interest him — a not uncommon problem among active young minds. Nonetheless, he went to Cambridge and, at the age of twenty-two, was made a Fellow of King's College. While at the university he conceived of the general plan for an intelligent computer, despite the fact that the computer itself was still little more than a few sketches on drawing boards. Later in this chapter we will see what happened to this hypothetical "Turing machine," as it was called.

Turing never married: perhaps fortunately, because life with him would probably have been an endless trial. He was, for example, addicted to games, chess in particular; and he introduced to chess a highly unorthodox variation. After making a move, a player had to jump up and run once around the building. If he returned before his opponent had moved, then he was permitted an extra turn. Most likely Turing won extra moves often, for he was a skilled runner and continued to compete in track events even after a leg injury slowed him down permanently.

Like many other brilliant adults, he retained a strong childish streak in his personality. Turing never lost his taste for childhood entertainments; juvenile shows on the BBC delighted him. Many of his close friends were children, with whom he seemed to enjoy a better rapport than with adults.

Turing's interests covered many fields of knowledge. He was an amateur musician, though of no great promise, and at one point he developed a passion for vertebrate embryology. But his first love remained mathematics, and he was fascinated by the technology of handling numbers: a technology that led him to conceive of the Turing machine.

The Turing machine was, in a sense, a universal computer, a theoretical construction like von Neumann's automata. As Turing imagined it, the Turing machine would consist of a device that scanned an endless tape marked off in squares, in the manner of motion-picture film. Each square is either blank or marked with a few symbols. The Turing machine reads the tape square by square, and can advance or reverse the tape one square at a time. It can also print or wipe out symbols on the tape as needed.

Turing was able to demonstrate, hypothetically, that a machine like his, capable of only these few simple operations, could also handle *any* job of computing, so long as the problem could be solved by computation (some cannot) and could be expressed in binary code.

Turing proposed his machine in 1937. A few years later he had an opportunity to help build a real computer for use in the fight against Hitler.

The British, battling for their lives against the military might of the Third Reich, knew they had to find a way to break German codes. Some system was needed to unscramble messages from the German high command. And if anyone could help build such a system, Turing was the person to do it. Exactly what he helped to build is still a secret, but the British code-breakers knew it as the "Eastern Goddess," a large and mysterious-looking machine vaguely reminiscent in form of a bronze Buddha. The Goddess swallowed coded messages from the German commanders and spat the orders back out as a decoded text.*

The Goddess was, of course, a lifesaver, but Britain also had to pay a price in lives for having to keep Goddess a secret. Because the British could not risk making its existence known to the Germans, Britain had to avoid doing anything that might give the secret code-breaking system away. And once that exigency doomed a city. When German radio transmissions were deciphered to reveal a planned attack on the cathedral city of Coventry, the British were helpless to plan countermeasures; any special effort to fend off the assault on Coventry would tip off the Nazis that their attack plans had been found out, and the Goddess would be a secret no longer. So the British were forced to leave Coventry open and unprotected against the Luftwaffe's bombs. Coventry, including its cathedral, was destroyed: a high, but to the British leaders acceptable, price to pay for the Goddess's continued aid. Today Coventry has a new cathedral, a glass-sided affair completed in the 1960s; the charred and broken hulk of the old cathedral remains as a reminder of how much a computer did to win the war for the Allies.

Turing served his country well, and after the war he returned to the service of science. At Britain's National Physical Laboratory he worked for a time on a device called the Automatic Computing En-

---

* Among the other British code-breakers in World War II was Ian Fleming, who later achieved fame as the creator of James Bond.

gine (ACE). But as he worked on that project, his mind kept returning time and again to a certain question: can machines think?

In 1947 he produced a paper dealing with that question. Its title was "Intelligent Machinery," and in it Turing said, in effect, that yes, machines could think. In fact machines — the bundles of nerves we refer to as brains — are thinking right now. And if natural machines can harbor thoughts, then in theory there is no reason why artificial machines should be barren of mental processes.

Consider, said Turing, the human baby. Its mental machine is largely unprogrammed. The baby has a lot to learn and understand before it can take its place in the world. So we educate — that is, program — this little thinking machine over a period of a few years. We fill the child's mind with facts and with what computer scientists call "heuristic guidelines": rules of thumb that will help the child learn to make commonsense judgments. The Ten Commandments are heuristic guidelines. So are all the old copybook maxims such as "It is never too late to mend," or "Honesty is the best policy." Eventually, with luck, the child is programmed in such a way that he or she will be able to fit in with the rest of society.

Turing saw computers as unprogrammed brains, much like those of human infants, though less sophisticated. With the right kind of "education," Turing believed, it was perfectly possible that a machine could be made intelligent. One merely had to find the right kind of teaching process.

Turing had a variety of tasks in mind for his proposed thinking machine. At first, he suggested putting it to work on intellectual games like chess and tic-tac-toe. The machine, Turing thought, could solve the problems involved in such games (say, whether or not to sacrifice a knight in hopes of getting the other player's queen) by a sophisticated search procedure. The machine would run through in its mind — or what passed for its mind — all the possible solutions to a given problem, and settle at last on the one best suited to the requirements of the situation at hand.

Later researchers discovered that the search procedure was not as quick and easy as Turing seemed to think it would be. Indeed, it turned out that human thinking machines solve problems in quite a different way, which will be discussed in a later chapter.

But at the time Turing's proposal sounded reasonable — to some thinkers, at least. Others were skeptical. Still others were shocked, outraged, and even apoplectic at the idea of an artificial thinking machine. Machines with *minds!* Poppycock, said Turing's critics, in much the same tone as the cynics who, a few decades earlier, had decided that human beings would never fly because they were never meant to fly.

Turing expected that many followers of his work would object to his views. And objections there were aplenty. Yet Turing had responses for each objection. For example: "Machines aren't conscious!" That depends on how one defines consciousness; depending on which criteria one selects, an egg timer may qualify as a conscious being — while humans may look as unconscious as rocks and stones.

"Humans have souls — machines don't!" All right, what *is* the soul? How do we define it? And most important of all, how do we demonstrate its existence and show that it has to do with intelligence? Unless and until all these things are done, it makes no sense to rule out the possibility of intelligent machines, on the basis of their lacking "souls."

"Machines can't be creative!" Here "creative" means capable of producing enduring works of art, music, verse, et cetera. Machines as yet are incapable of writing an *Eroica* or a *War and Peace*. But so are the vast majority of humans. Does that mean that most of us are as stupid as mere machines?

Turing had little patience with contrived definitions of what intelligence is or is not. He realized that trying to define intelligence precisely, in terms that apply in all situations, was a hopeless task. Instead he proposed a *test*. Today it is known universally as the Turing test, even though Turing himself referred to it as the "imitation game."

Basically, the Turing test is this. Suppose you are seated in a closed room, and your only means of communication with the outside world is a telegraph or a teletype or computer display terminal, or some other device for sending and receiving printed messages. And you *do* communicate with some other party at the other end of the line. He, she, or it keeps exchanging messages with you, and your job is to figure out whether your correspondent is a human being or merely a cunningly programmed machine.

Imagine that the dialogue goes as follows:

Good morning, says the other party.

Good morning, *you reply.* Who are you?

Who wants to know?

If we're going to have a conversation, I'd like to know who you are.

I'm a conversationalist.

That's not very helpful.

I can't help that.

You could tell me your name. That would help.

Sorry.

Can you tell me anything else about yourself?

Yes, I can.

Please do.

I don't want to.

Why not?

I don't have to tell you.

What is the square root of sixteen?

Sorry.

This exchange is inconclusive. You might be dealing with a machine programmed with a limited set of responses — and therefore unintelligent — or with an intelligent human who for some reason is trying to confuse you. But if the answers keep coming in this stupid, unresponsive vein for hours on end, the chances are probably better than fifty-fifty that you are dealing with a dumb machine.

On the other hand, suppose you get responses like this:

What do you think of Sinclair Lewis?

Love him. He's my favorite twentieth-century American novelist.

Which of his novels have you read?

All of them.

Okay, then tell me which was his very first novel.

Hike and the Aeroplane.

Which is your favorite?

Babbitt.

Who is it who appears in Babbitt's dreams?

The Fairy Child.

And what's that insulting expression his son has for him?

"Goo-goo," I believe.

What do you think marks Lewis most strongly as a novelist?

Definitely not his mastery of plot. His novels were strung together rather than plotted. I guess his most outstanding virtue as an author is his mastery of detail. One little detail can tell you so much about a Lewis character. Take Elmer Gantry, for example. . . .

By now it is clear that someone or something intelligent is on the other end of the wire. These responses demonstrate a thorough knowledge of the subject under discussion, combined with a keen analytical sense. Therefore, the chance of these replies coming from an unintelligent being is virtually zero. And if the respondent happens to be a machine, one would almost be forced to admit that the machine is intelligent.

The Turing test for intelligence, then, is this: *If a machine can convince you that its behavior is intelligent, then its behavior really is intelligent.* In the absence of a neat, cut-and-dried definition of intelligence, Turing's test is probably the best criterion we will get.

All right, assuming a machine can be made intelligent, what is the key to making it intelligent? Turing believed the answer was information: lots and lots of it. The more data a machine had stored in its memory, the more successful its searches for desired information would be, and the more intelligence it would show.

But would we recognize a machine's intelligence *as* intelligence? Turing was willing to admit that a machine might be bright by its own standards but abysmally stupid by ours, and vice versa, because ours might not be the only possible kind of intelligence. "May not machines," Turing asked, "carry out something that ought to be described as thinking but that is very different from what a man does?"

The very words *think* and *thought* struck Turing as highly arbitrary and artificial — so much so, he once said, that they made the question of whether or not a machine can think "too meaningless to deserve discussion." Still, he discussed it. And he expressed a belief that "at the end of the century the use of words and general educated opinion will have altered so much that one will be able to speak of machines thinking without expecting to be contradicted." As we will see later, "educated opinion" is not quite to that point yet, but appears to be getting there.

Turing's goal was to build an artificial brain in which the fire of intelligence could be stoked, so to speak, by careful programming. But Turing knew little about the workings of the brain. He was a mathematician, not a physiologist, and he had only the vaguest ideas about how the human brain operates. He did know that machines can duplicate the workings of other organs such as muscles and bones, so why not the brain as well? If our natural computer can house intelligence, thought Turing, then an intellect might live just as cozily in an artificial brain built along the same lines.

The analogy between brains and machines was slippery, because Turing, in his ignorance of brain functions, tried something similar to equating apples with pineapples. They have a certain similarity: both have the phonic segment "apple" in them. But pineapples will not grow on trees, because they and apples represent two very different kinds of plants. In much the same manner, Turing tried to place the fruit of intelligence where it might not belong — within the circuits of a computer.

But Turing's vision was inspiring, and it dominates many areas of research into artificial intelligence (AI) to this day. Turing himself might have become a dominant figure in the modern AI community, but death intervened.

What drove Alan Turing, a highly successful young scientist with a brilliant record behind him and most likely an equally brilliant one ahead, to take his own life? Though no one can probe the motives of a dead man, strong rumor had it that Turing was homosexual, at a time when British law still carried heavy penalties for the "crime" of homosexuality. Very possibly Turing, faced with the exposure of his sexual preference, opted for death rather than face the wrath of the law and a sanctimonious public. Oscar Wilde had his career ruined by British homophobia, and one can understand why Turing might have preferred suicide to such a sentence.

In a tragically short lifetime, Turing managed to set the course of AI research for the next two decades. The machine he described in his writings, and the intelligence test that he provided for it, formed the basis for much of the research on artificial intelligence almost up to the present day.

Checkmate! | 10

Visionary thoughts like Turing's were commonplace in AI research during the early 1950s, as computer experts tackled the problem of "engineering" intelligence into a machine. And following Turing's recommendations, they tried first to program computers to play games.

Games had several things to recommend them as targets for early AI efforts. Games are played according to rules, so that if one can give a machine some understanding of those rules, then the machine ought to be able to play the game competently, as a human would. Also, because games follow definite rules, they offered a convenient way to tell just how successful "intelligent" programming was. If a computer won more than 50 or 60 percent of its matches against a human opponent, then one could say with some assurance that the program was a success. Just chalk up wins and losses on the board, and tally up the results.

But best of all, game-playing AI programs seemed to offer a road toward attainment of humanlike intelligence. Look at so-called intelligent people. What do they do for recreation? Among other things, they play intellectual games like chess. If a computer could master games of this kind, then wouldn't it be well on the way to developing what we would call an intellect?

Perhaps it would. But this line of reasoning has its flaws. There is quite a lot more to intelligence than the successful playing of games; otherwise our greatest savants might be shortstops and fullbacks. So it makes little sense to equate skill at such games with intellectual prowess in general. This is somewhat like saying that because a bird makes a beautiful song, the bird will be capable of writing grand opera as well.

The early optimism of AI advocates would be dampened in short order. But high hopes were widespread in the 1950s following the successes of some AI programs, such as the one developed by Dr. Arthur Samuel of Stanford University.

Samuel chose checkers as the game for computer play. Checkers seemed reasonably easy to learn (it lacks many of the complicated rules that make chess a challenge) and therefore suitable to programming into a machine. So Samuel proposed in 1947 that, as a demonstration, a computer be programmed for checkers to help raise funds for a new high-powered computer at the University of Illinois, where Samuel was then on the faculty.

After throwing himself into the task of devising a program for this game, Samuel soon found the job was more complicated and difficult than it had appeared at first. There was, for one thing, the problem of making the computer look ahead. Any competent human player tries to foresee, at least one or two steps in advance, which plays are open to him and to his opponent. But the farther ahead one looks, the more complicated the problem becomes. Each next move makes possible more moves, which in turn make possible still *more* moves — and after a few steps forward, the mind simply cannot keep track of all the possibilities. Very soon one's options are ramifying like the dendrites on a nerve cell.

This kind of forward-looking calculation takes time, even for an electronic computer, because the computer — if programmed on the Turing model — has to consider the future moves one by one, for a total of perhaps a few hundred moves. But Samuel persevered and, by 1961, was getting impressive results. The checkers program he devised came to play a better game than its creator did. The program reached the Master's level and drew high praise from the human players who opposed it; one checkers champion said he had not faced such skilled competition in years.

Chess, as might be expected, turned out to be a less tractable game than checkers, because the structure of chess is much more complicated. Instead of merely moving identical wooden discs around the board, as in checkers, the chess player has to manipulate several different kinds of pieces, ranging from the little pawns to the powerful queen. And to make matters still more daunting, there are times when one piece can substitute for another: a rook for a queen, for instance.

In a typical chess game there are so many possible moves (something on the order of 10^{120}, or one followed by 120 zeros), there is no way for a computer to look ahead far enough to figure all of them. If a computer had started working on that task at the moment the universe was created, then the computer would still be calculating, and would probably have work yet to finish when the universe finally winds down, billions of years from now, when earth and space assume a common temperature.

Chess-playing programs were therefore equipped with rules that the programmers hoped would enable the machines to concentrate on the most promising avenues of play, thus avoiding the need to figure out thousands on thousands of potential moves beforehand. These heuristic rules, distilled from centuries of human experience, were meant to steer the computer's operations in the right direction — but more importantly, they allowed the computer to learn from its successes and mistakes. If the machine committed a disastrous error, it would know better than to make the same blunder twice. Intimidating as this project was, programmers hoped to have electronic computers playing chess on the expert level within a few years.*

---

* That hope was shot down at the 1982 National Conference on Artificial Intelligence in Pittsburgh, where human players trounced computers soundly in a three-day competition. Four computers faced off against four human chess experts, who established a 9-to-3 point advantage over the machines in the first three rounds of play, and won eight out of twelve games. The computers won two games; the others were draws. The machines were slower on the uptake than expected; one human

Chess is a logical game. If I make this move, then the other fellow can do such and such to me. And if computers could be programmed for chess play, then more complex and formal logic was within their grasp as well — at least in theory. Working on that principle, programmers started trying to make AI systems into what Thomas Huxley had hoped to see in human minds: cold, clear "logic engines." The most impressive result of this effort was a program called Logic Theorist, which was unveiled at a conference on artificial intelligence that was held at Dartmouth College in 1956.

Logic Theorist was designed to take logical propositions and prove them, point by point. And the program did just that — did it so well, in fact, that on one occasion Logic Theorist went two human geniuses one better, and scored a first in mathematics. The humans were the authors of *Principia Mathematica*, Bertrand Russell and Alfred North Whitehead. Their monumental work on mathematical logic taxes the minds of most professional mathematicians, and so anyone who came up with a proof missed by Whitehead and Russell in their book would probably be acclaimed as a genius.

Logic Theorist *did* devise a proof that they had missed. So on one level at least, Logic Theorist was the intellectual equivalent of two of the greatest logicians of all time. Moreover, Logic Theorist satisfied one of the classical tests of intelligence. It was unpredictable. One could not always tell just what the program would do under given conditions. That proof for the Whitehead-Russell theorem, for instance, was unexpected. The machine had not been told to look for it, but had devised it anyway. Logic Theorist's behavior was more than a little reminiscent of the young Pascal, working out Euclid's discoveries in geometry for himself.

Early triumphs like these naturally tended to make AI specialists enthusiastic about prospects for the future. In 1957, two of Logic Theorist's creators predicted that in the next decade computers would become reasonably skilled composers of music and would discover and prove other significant theorems in higher math.

---

player defeated a computer by using the very same move that another human had already used to win a game with the same computer!

But there were no computerized Chopins by the 1970s. The evolution of "intelligent" computers had taken quite different directions, among them the development of "smart" robots. Humans had joined an extension of their bodies — robot arms — with an extension of their minds, programmable "smart" computers that, in effect, put an artificial brain behind those metal limbs. Two trends in the evolution of human technology (and, through it, humankind) had come together in a new device, the "thinking" robot.

It was a tremendous breakthrough in invention. And in much the same way that the Cro-Magnons' superior wit and technology helped to drive their Neanderthal rivals into obsolescence and extinction, modern humans with smart robots at their sides are already encroaching on the domains of computer-unaided people. The outcome may be one of the greatest social upheavals — or catastrophes — in history.

Rotwang's Robot | 11

The scene: a darkened laboratory.

The place: a large city.

In the middle of the lab sits a chair on a pedestal. In the chair sits the metal image of a human being: a robot. And nearby, inside a transparent coffin, lies a young woman asleep with electrodes affixed to her body. Bustling about the lab with hurricane energy is a white-haired man clad in a long dark robe like that of a medieval sorcerer. On one hand he wears a black glove to signify that the hand is artificial; he lost the original in an accident some years before.

He throws a switch, and all around the laboratory, equipment starts to spin, glow, and crackle with electrical discharges. Then he throws another switch — and the seated metal figure starts to undergo a weird transformation. Electrical coronas and bizarre displays of light surround the metal figure. Luminescent rings of energy move upward and downward along the gleaming body. But for what purpose?

Soon we see. As we watch, the mechanism reproduces the face and form of the sleeping woman on the body of a robot. The result, a beautiful, human-looking robotrix.

The berobed scientist and his robot offspring are two of the characters in Fritz Lang's famous 1927 motion picture *Metropolis*. The story of a future clash between labor and management, *Metropolis* is seldom seen today, although in its time it was as popular as George Lucas's space epics are now. Lang was inspired to film *Metropolis,* he said in an interview many years later, while on a boat approaching New York City. The sight of the city's skyscrapers evoked in him a vision of an even more impressive future city, controlled by a single man, John Masterman (Joh Fredersen in some versions), and kept running by the labors of countless oppressed workers.

In the movie, Masterman is dissatisfied with his workers' performance and starts wondering how to do away with human labor altogether. So he calls on Rotwang, his chief scientist, to design and build an artificial worker, a robot that will never tire, nor need sleep and food.

Rotwang says it can be done. At Masterman's order, the scientist sets to work on the project, while the master of Metropolis returns to his executive suite, pondering how the robot laborer will improve his fortunes.

Soon, Masterman thinks, the flesh-and-blood worker will be obsolete. The city's machinery will be run even more efficiently than before! To a plutocrat like Masterman, the thought of a tireless work force is heavenly.

But Rotwang's imagination gets the better of him, and — for reasons that are never quite made clear in the movie — he decides a mere metal automaton is not enough. So he gives his machine the appearance of a striking young woman — with disastrous consequences.

The beautified robot becomes a Joan of Arc figure and leads the workers in rebellion. Rotwang's robotrix is destroyed, along with the scientist and much of the city, in the ensuing conflict. But eventually the bosses and the workers are reconciled, and John Masterman concludes a truce with the workers.

Metropolis left something to be desired as drama, in part because Lang and his wife, Thea von Harbou, who wrote the story, inserted an improbable love affair between a girl of the lower class and John Masterman's son. But Lang and von Harbou did create a powerful picture of what automation — specifically, a programmable robot — might do to labor and to society as a whole. One message of *Metropolis* is that the "blessing" of mechanical servants might turn out to be a catastrophe in disguise.

That message has particular relevance to society now, for we are on the same course as John Masterman and his fictional city. In the process of extending our minds and bodies, we have created a generation of computerized robots that are unlike any tools invented before. They are likely to make many human workers obsolete, just as the unarmored fishes outperformed their armored cousins in the late Paleozoic. The consequences are likely to be highly unpleasant, if not calamitous, for the industrial nations in the years ahead.

Robots, equipped with computer "brains," are being programmed with elementary reasoning skills that will allow them to handle many factory jobs just as well as a human worker, if not better. There are, for example, robots with "sorting" abilities.

Take a set of objects laid out in some given order, and rearrange them. Then tell a smart robot to put the things back in the right order. The robot can and will comply, thanks to an ingenious system of recognizing objects: a "silhouette vision system" that uses a TV camera and various pieces of computer equipment in about the same way that a human would use his or her eyes and brain.

Suppose you have a set of spoons, ranging in size from a tiny sugar spoon to a large spoon used for serving salads. Originally they are lined up, left to right, in order of increasing size. All the spoons are stainless steel, and no two have the same dimensions.

Now take the spoons into the dining room. Put a dark cloth on the table, and scatter the spoons on it, so that they fall onto the cloth in random orientations. Then call in a robot with a silhouette vision system to put the spoons back in proper order.*

The robot looks at the mess on the table, its TV camera producing an image of the spoons. Because the spoons are lying on a dark

---

* More than likely the robot would be stationary, and you would have to bring the spoons to it. But portable "smart" robots may be just around the corner, and by the end of the century the ponderous robot mechanisms of today may have been reduced so much in weight and volume that they will fit into a suitcase.

background, there is plenty of contrast, and the robot can see them all clearly.

Next the spoons are silhouetted. With the computer's help, the robot's vision system determines a threshold value of brightness somewhere between the gleam of the spoons and the deep, rich tones of the cloth. This value helps the computer distinguish the spoons from the background: an important prerequisite for the next step, which is called outlining.

Using brightness and darkness as a guide, the system picks out the outlines of the spoons. In this case outlining is easy because the bright spoons lie on such a dark field. Starting at the upper left-hand corner, just like a person reading a page of this book, the system looks over the image and picks out silhouette borders, as the TV scanner moves down the picture line by line.

When the computer encounters an edge — that is, a transition from dark to light or vice versa — the machine stops briefly and checks adjacent points on the line above, to see if this edge belongs to one noted earlier. If no other edge points turn up, the computer assumes a new edge has appeared, and will keep an electronic eye out for more edge points on the next line of the scan. Soon the scanning is done, and the system is able to map out the edges of all the spoons. (This outlining procedure seems very similar to what goes on in our brains when we see some object in sharp contrast to its background. The first thing our eyes do is to flit about the edges of the object, outlining it to aid in recognition.)

Now comes the "brainiest" part of the operation: figuring out which spoon is which. For humans this process is simple. Our programming allows us to merely glance at the spoons and say, "Well, there's the big salad spoon up there, and here's the little sugar spoon down here" — and so on. But the machine must take a more formal and mathematical approach, because it lacks the nonmathematical "shorthand" of our mental programs.

The computer figures out the "geometric center of gravity" of each spoon's silhouette. This is the midpoint of the silhouette, at which half the spoon's area lies on either side of the point, whether you divide the spoon lengthwise down the handle or crosswise through the handle. But the center of gravity also serves as the mid-point for something besides the silhouette: an equivalent ellipse. The computer uses this ellipse to gauge the relative sizes of the spoons. For each spoon the computer generates an ellipse equal in area to that particular spoon, and oriented along the spoon's long axis. The computer also determines the orientation of the spoon by checking the tilt of the ellipse with respect to a reference framework built into its programming.

At this point the computer knows how big the objects in front of it are, and how they are positioned. Now to find out just *what* the things are. The machine compares the silhouette of each spoon with a reference silhouette in its memory. If the two images look reasonably similar (not necessarily a perfect match), then the computer makes an identification: "SPOON." The computer's arms proceed to pick up the scattered spoons and replace them all in the desired order. And if you try to confuse the computer by tossing a fork or a steak knife onto the table, chances are the computer will be smart enough to detect the trick, decide "NOT SPOON," and leave the unwanted bits of cutlery alone.

How close a correspondence is needed for a successful identification? The computer has a "tally sheet" of features for each thing it is expected to identify. Every item on the list is worth a certain number of points, which programmers call "weighting factors." If the total number of points for some object tops a predetermined value, the machine goes ahead and identifies that object as the one logged in its memory.

One well-known vaudeville routine was built around this same kind of "checklist" procedure. One of the characters would say, "If it *looks* like an elephant . . . *smells* like an elephant . . . and *sounds* like an elephant . . . it probably *is* an elephant!" As it happened, his list of features was a little faulty, and something he identified as an elephant turned out to be most definitely *not* an elephant — much to his chagrin. But if even humans can make serious errors in this kind of matching game, then we ought to be doubly impressed that a computer can do it so well.

Systems like this one are not very bright by human standards. But high intelligence is not needed for many of the jobs that such robots might be assigned. On the contrary, low intelligence can be a definite plus in many jobs, for it makes the robot unable to err from carelessness. Whereas humans have active and imaginative minds that can wander after a few hours on a repetitive and boring job, a robot can keep its vestigial mind directly on its given task for long periods. That is one reason why more and more robots are entering the workplace. They are assembling cars for us, baking our food, refining our petroleum, bottling our beverages. Here are some other tasks that "smart" robots are likely to take over from us in the reasonably near future:

• Working in mines is a grueling task, as anyone knows who has spent time in coal-producing regions, or has read George Orwell's vivid descriptions of conditions in British mines, in *The Road to Wigan Pier*. Robots could take over some of the most trying and hazardous parts of mining operations from humans. The robots might even do the job much more efficiently. The human body did not evolve specifically to fit conditions found in narrow tunnels far underground.* Robots, on the other hand, could be designed exclusively to work under those conditions; they could then labor tirelessly in hot, cramped spaces, oblivious to heat, swirling dust, and toxic gases. Via a TV hookup, supervisors on the surface could keep an eye on what the machines were doing, and call a halt to their digging if anything looked suspicious on the monitors.

Mining robots need not be restricted to the land, either. They could perform their labors just as well at the bottom of the sea, scooping up the metal-rich nodules that cover many stretches of the ocean floor. Here the temperatures are close to freezing, and

---

* On the contrary, we appear to have evolved in rather spacious and airy environments: namely treetops and open grasslands. Some biologists have suggested this is one reason why so many of us are subject to claustrophobia: life in enclosed spaces works at odds with the ancient primate programming that still lingers in our brains. The environments in which we evolved may also account for "color psychology," our responses to various colors. Blue and green surroundings, for example, tend to calm an excited person down — perhaps because those are the colors of treetops and sky, and take us back subconsciously to our homes of long ago.

pressures may reach several tons per square inch. Humans could never work in this hostile environment without all manner of elaborate and expensive life-support equipment; but a deep-diving robot could handle the job easily, and for a fraction of the cost of human labor, returning mineral riches to the surface in an endless and highly profitable stream.

Robots might even mine the seawater itself — not for dissolved minerals such as gold, which are present in seawater at such low concentrations that extracting them would be impractical, but rather for the hydrogen and oxygen that make up the water.

The physicist Freeman Dyson has suggested building a fleet of robot vessels to cruise the oceans, using solar energy to "crack" water into hydrogen and oxygen and to make other useful and simple chemicals from the seas. When their storage tanks were full, the robots would then head automatically for the nearest discharge point to unload their cargo, and afterward return to sea for another load.

· Exploration of new and unknown environments is a risky business, whether here on earth or out in space. Staggering amounts of money are needed to send out human scouting teams and to provide equipment to support them. Deep-sea explorers have to have submarines; astronauts require expensive space capsules; and even a relatively minor mountain-climbing expedition may consume millions of dollars.

In many such cases, unmanned, "smart" probes would be a better investment. They could be sent out without the many pieces of support equipment needed by human explorers, and if lost they could be replaced for relatively little money. Thus far, however, the big problem with unmanned vehicles has been their lack of intelligence; they can hardly do anything without an explicit command from their human masters. The order may take a long time to transmit, and even longer to reach the probe, especially on deep-space missions where astronomical distances are involved. And the slightest delay may spell disaster for the machine.

Imagine a remote-controlled vehicle scouting the surface of Mars. A four-wheeled contraption with a TV camera in front, it rolls slowly over the Martian landscape, peering ahead at the rocky terrain, while controllers back on earth watch the view transmitted to them by the rover's TV camera. What they see on earth, the camera picked up fifteen minutes before; it takes that long for a signal, traveling at the velocity of light, to make the trip to earth from Mars.

Suddenly the picture shows a frightening image: what appears to be a deep chasm yawning directly in the rover's path. The humans try frantically to halt the vehicle before it tumbles over the edge, but they fail. By the time the picture was received, the rover had already rolled over the chasm rim to its destruction. Confirmation of the machine's doom arrives a few seconds later, when the picture on the monitor at mission control lurches and then vanishes in a shower of static, leaving only a dead gray blur on the screen.

This is what a "dumb," remote-controlled machine might do. A "smart" rover, however, would be much less likely to get into that kind of trouble. Programmed to watch for potential hazards like crevasses or exceedingly steep slopes, the intelligent rover could avoid obstacles and pitfalls in its path, without the need for constant shepherding from mission control. Intelligent rovers could make mission control's job much easier and might also save the taxpayers billions of dollars by cutting the risk of accidents.

• Intelligent machines may revolutionize agriculture in years to come. Already U.S. and Canadian farms are automated to a remarkable degree, as in the tomato fields of California, where a single machine, traveling slowly down the rows of tomato plants, can handle every step of the harvesting operation, from uprooting the plants to basketing the picked tomatoes. Under the guidance of perhaps one or two operators, the machine handles the work of a dozen or more human pickers, and does it much more neatly and quickly. Crop scientists have even bred a special kind of tomato to suit the specifications of the harvesting machine.

If agriculture can be automated this far, there ought to be no problem in carrying automation just a bit farther by putting intelligent computers in charge of the whole procedure. In the near future, computerized "farmers" may carry out much of our food production, from the planting of seeds to the canning of the crops.

• Many jobs in manufacturing are so dangerous, degrading, or debilitating that humans prefer to avoid them. These jobs, such as working in extremely hot environments or in places made hazardous by toxic chemicals or radioactivity, could be done by programmable robots, thus saving men and women the risk of blindness, mutilation, or asphyxiation. Indeed, the use of robots in industry is already well under way, and here the Japanese lead the world. Western visitors to Japan gape in awe when they see automated factories where robots do virtually all the work. Humans seldom have to lift a wrench or even tighten a screw. At one Nissan automobile plant near Tokyo, for example, fewer than seventy workers are able, with the aid of computer-assisted robots, to produce an average of some thirteen hundred cars daily.

This is high technology with a vengeance. And other nations, impressed by Japan's commitment to robotizing the workplace, are determined to catch up with the Japanese as quickly as possible. The United States in particular is eager to join the rush toward robot technology, and advancing that technology is the goal of numerous robot research projects under way at schools such as MIT, Stanford, Carnegie-Mellon, the University of Rhode Island, and others.

The Charles Stark Draper Laboratory in Cambridge, Massachusetts, for example, has come up with a robot capable of assembling a seventeen-piece auto alternator in just under three minutes. The robot does everything a human could, right down to tightening the screws.

Across the country in California, Stanford University is trying to give robot "fingers" something like a sense of touch. That capability would come in handy for assembly-line robots, many of which cannot now tell whether they are holding something tightly enough to crush it, or so loosely that it might fall to the floor. The Stanford robot represents a giant step forward in manipulator design, roughly equivalent to the evolution of the opposable thumb in humans. Stanford's robot can move its hand without moving the entire arm — a feat that most other robots are unable to accomplish. The fingers of the robot "hand" are connected by cable to servomechanisms farther down the arm: an improvement over other designs, which require the servos to be mounted right on the fingers.

A manually dexterous robot with a computer "brain" would be a godsend to manufacturers, and engineers are already well on the way to computer-robotizing whole assembly lines. Computerized "foremen" could direct large segments of factory operations, altering work schedules to compensate for a machine breaking down somewhere along the line. The machines could even be programmed to add little personal touches to products, so as to make them more individual and thus counteract the cookie-cutter sameness of many manufactured goods. If Mr. Jones wants an automobile with racing stripes, while Ms. Brown prefers the same car minus that feature, computers in an auto assembly plant could accommodate both orders easily: just tell the robots down on the floor to make those minor variations on the cars. Thus a "smart" assembly line could help keep the customer happy and the manufacturer in the black.

As far as employers are concerned, robots have an edge over human employees in almost every way. Just look at the budget sheet. Roughly 60 percent of the budget of most firms is devoured by payrolls. A human worker must be paid a salary, year in and year out. A robot doesn't get paid. Just buy it, install it, and set it to work. In a couple of years the robot can pay back the cost of its purchase, solely by cutting payrolls. And the savings to the employer should increase in the years ahead, as new technologies drive down the cost of robots and expand their capabilities.

Moreover, robots can make labor relations more peaceful, by getting rid of human labor. Machines don't organize unions. They never call in sick, or require paid holidays and lunch hours and coffee breaks. A computer will never turn to federal regulators and blow the whistle on unsavory corporate practices. Computers and robots are quiet, tireless, dependable, and docile. Those are precisely the qualities that employers like to see in workers, and also the qualities that robots can provide. So, more and more robots are likely to take jobs from humans in the next few years, possibly creating an unemployment crisis that will make the Hoover years seem like paradise.

Where the robot revolution is concerned, we are talking not about small and localized labor woes, such as a few farm workers put out of their jobs by the purchase of a new crop-harvesting machine. We are forced to consider instead the loss of *whole categories of jobs,* involving enough workers to fill the nation's biggest cities.

How many employees stand to be replaced by "smart" machines? Estimates vary, but one figure published in *Business Week* in 1982 puts the potential job losses at twenty-two to twenty-five million individuals. Twenty-five million: that is roughly the population of southern New England, or of Virginia and both Carolinas. Imagine everyone between the Potomac and the Georgia border out of work, or every employee in America's ten largest metropolitan areas getting a pink slip, and you have some idea of the number of jobs involved. Picture all of Boston, New York City, Chicago, San Francisco, Los Angeles, and Detroit standing in the welfare line, everyone replaced by robots.

Keep in mind also that not all the workers thrown off their job will wear blue collars. As machines grow ever brighter and more versatile, white-collar employees will have to worry about *their* jobs, too. Bookkeepers and accountants will be shoved aside to make room for expert systems. And it may be only a few years until companies can replace human secretaries with computer systems programmed with "natural language capability," the ability to communicate in plain English.

Not far in the future, the boss may come in to work and find no one in the office to greet him. The human staff was fired long ago. The receptionist's chair and desk are gone. Now the room is occupied only by a few plants and a small table with a computer terminal on it. The boss presses a key on the computer, and on the display screen the computer prints out its morning report:

HELLO, MR. PARKER. HOPE YOU'RE FEELING WELL TODAY.
YOUR SCHEDULE FOR TODAY, MONDAY, MARCH 23, IS:
8:00 A.M. MEETING WITH MR. JONES TO DISCUSS AD CAMPAIGN.
9:00 A.M. MEETING WITH MR. HOWARD TO DISCUSS BUSINESS INSURANCE POLICIES.
10:00 A.M. EXPECT CALL FROM MS. WHITE CONCERNING BANK LOAN.

Et cetera. The computer could be programmed to take incoming messages via electronic mail and display them on a screen, ranked in order of importance. For instance, a call from a bank president would undoubtedly take priority over a friendly message from an old Harvard classmate who just happened to be passing through town. A special "filter" program could even be installed to intercept "junk" messages.

A speech-adapted office computer could answer many phone calls with appropriate replies. ("I'm sorry. Mr. Parker is not available at the moment. But if you would care to leave your name, number, and company affiliation, Mr. Parker will return your call. . . . ") Setting up appointments would be no great problem, either. The computer could be programmed with an understanding of what and who is or is not important. A meeting with a visiting corporation chief, for example, had best be slotted for the most impressive conference room or restaurant available. That visiting friend from Harvard, on the other hand, could be met over a hot dog in the parking lot.

A whole system like this might be had for no more than the annual salaries of two or three secretaries, and would last for years. Even more appealing to employers is the thought that the computer would count as machinery and therefore could be written off on the corporation's tax return.

So white-collar workers no longer may safely assume that their jobs are safe from automation. The specter of "computer unemployment" may haunt even middle-level executives in the next few years, as computers with special decision-making programs become available. In that event, those whimsical signs often seen in offices — "Remember, you could be replaced by a computer" — may not seem funny much longer.

Whenever conversation turns to topics like these, a sinister word is likely to pop up: "Luddite." The Luddites were early victims of technological unemployment. British factory workers cast from their jobs by automation in the first decade of the nineteenth century, the Luddites were furious and desperate men, and with good reason: they had been underpaid and overworked to start with, and the loss of their jobs to clanking machines was more than they could bear peaceably. To arms, the Luddites decided, and smash the machines!

Smash them they did, in a series of insurrections that lasted from 1811 to 1815. The rebels' figurehead was a mythical worker called

Ned Ludd, or "King Ludd" when the rioters were in an exalted mood. But their ardor and their imaginary king did the Luddites no good against the armed might of the real king; the government put down the uprising brutally, sending out against the Luddites an army bigger than the Duke of Wellington had for his campaign against Napoleon's troops in Spain. The undisciplined Luddites stood no chance against the guns and bayonets of the Crown. Peace was restored, but only at a tremendous price in blood; King Ludd vanished into the history books; and Britain's industrial revolution was made secure. In the process, however, millions of Britons were condemned to lives of misery, poverty, and brutal working conditions as mere slaves of machines. While the upper classes raked in wealth as never before, the lower classes descended into the nightmare that Dickens depicted so vividly: a hell of servitude to pieces of metal and their owners, the Bounderbys and the Gradgrinds, who built the "dark Satanic mills" of Blake's poem that turned London into so many grimy piles of stone. Such was the cost of technological Progress with a capital *P*.

Now the heirs of these factory owners, our John Mastermans in all their present-day incarnations, are seeking to install perfect workers — robot machines — in place of human labor. Can the Metropolis of today, our modern industrial society, somehow find new work for the hordes of men and women whom the new technology is likely to put on unemployment? Do we face neo-Luddite uprisings, mass rebellions of hopeless persons who feel they have nothing to lose by striking back at the machines that cost them their livelihood? And if those uprisings are put down by armed force, as the Luddite movement was, then what kind of society will be left to us after the shooting stops? Will we have a police state where the main job of law enforcement is to keep down a huge and permanent underclass? Will we turn into a crushing "tax state" in which those who have jobs are assessed higher and higher taxes to support a vast population of the chronically unemployed?

Perhaps computers can help us find some way out of the approaching crisis. With game theory and other tools of analysis to help, maybe we and our electronic mental extensions can find some acceptable minimax between the gains from automation and the losses from unemployment. But we will have to think of some solution soon, for Rotwang's icy fingers are already on our shoulders.

The "smart" machines described here are, as noted earlier, "stupid" by human standards. Yet these machines stand to have a mammoth impact on society. What, then, will be the effect of much *more highly evolved* AI systems?

The Needle's Eye | 12

Albert Einstein, toward the end of his life, is said to have turned to a young colleague at Princeton and remarked: "It all happened so *fast!*" Indeed it did. From the publication of Einstein's ideas on relativity theory to the explosion of the first A-bomb over Hiroshima — an event made possible by the famous matter-energy equation in Einstein's writings — less than fifty years elapsed. Physics and engineering had advanced, in one brief generation, from a few marks on paper to a fireball in the sky.

Much the same thing has happened in computer science. Only here the effects are even more dramatic. Nature took more than three billion years to turn inanimate chemicals here on earth into creatures with the intelligence of primitive insects; humans did essentially the same thing, with their invention, the computer, in less than half a century.

Computers might have evolved even faster, along Lamarckian guidelines and under human direction, but for one thing — a language barrier.

Our relatively sluggish, but generally superior, brand of thinking has proven very difficult to implant in computers, because a computer's "language" differs greatly from our own. Squeezing a camel through a needle's eye looks easy compared to the task of translating human-style thinking into "computerese."

And here we come to one of the thorniest problems in computer science — "knowledge representation."

Knowledge, like intelligence, is one of those things that seem so easy to define — and yet elude definition. We have a hard time breaking knowledge down into its components, because knowledge is after all a fruit of the human brain, and the brain's operations are still cloaked in mystery. So how do we feed our knowledge into the circuitry of a computer?

That question is rather like asking, "How do you prepare food?" There are so many different kinds of knowledge that no one approach is best for representing them all.

Some varieties of knowledge are easy to represent in computer language. Mathematical logic, for example, is perfectly suited to the computer's highly channeled way of "thinking." Mathematical logic has its own very precise symbology that can be converted easily into terms that a computer can handle. When a computer runs across the symbol "=," for instance, the computer can tell that whatever follows that symbol is equal to whatever precedes it.

But many other kinds of knowledge do not lend themselves so neatly to computer talk. This is one reason why computers have never developed the ability to write decent music or distinguished poetry: those activities require very subtle and special kinds of symbolism that the parallel-processing human "computer" can handle with ease, but that a machine doesn't know from Sunday.

Consider the musical expression (that is, symbol) *dolce*. A musician seeing that symbol on a score knows that it means to play the music in a particular way — "sweetly," so as to make the audience sigh, smile, and relax. This one little five-character symbol therefore contains a huge amount of information, very little of which can be encoded in digital form for a computer's edification.

We can, then, handle a much wider range of symbols than a computer can. Does this mean there is an unbridgeable chasm between our kind of thought and computers' "thinking"?

Maybe not. A few pages back, we saw how two very different kinds of systems — human beings and fuel-injection cars — start to look very similar, if you stand off at a distance and compare the cybernetic principles on which they work. Let's now do the same with people and computers.

The computer is a symbol-manipulating system. So is the human brain. You may never have thought of your brain in quite that way before, but both computers and brains are, on the highest, most intelligent level, just devices for juggling symbols. Symbols make up all the thoughts racing around your conscious mind, just as symbols compose all the statements that go into and issue from computers.

So maybe there is a way to make computers "think" more or less as we do — if we can find the right kinds of symbols for the computer to handle.

In the last couple of decades, machine-programming languages have grown ever more subtle and sophisticated, until now we can translate many of our mental concepts — love, hate, hunger, fear — into computerese, so that the machine can manipulate these symbols (without, of course, necessarily feeling the emotions behind them). Robots can even be commanded, in plain English words, to do things, because of this breakthrough in symbolism.

A good case in point is PLANNER, a language used in an "intelligent" system that we will examine shortly. PLANNER condenses lots of information into compact, single-word symbols. Suppose you want a robot to pick up something from a table and hand it to you. Using PLANNER, you could address the robot simply, as follows:

CLEARTOP: X
PICKUP: X
MOVEHAND (LOCATION: Y)

This sequence of commands tells the robot to pick up an object — say, a water glass — at point X on the tabletop, and pass it over to your waiting hand at point Y. Grasp the glass so that it won't fall, and then tell the robot:

OPENHAND

The robot lets go of the glass, and you are ready to fill it with water for a refreshing drink.

Imagine having to put commands like that into ones and zeros! But with the kind of symbolism PLANNER provides, communication between the human symbol-manipulator (the brain) and the robot symbol-manipulator (the computer) is relatively easy. In fact, computers and humans have been chattering away at each other, in plain English sentences, for more than a decade, thanks to programs like MIT's ELIZA.

ELIZA, the first "conversational" program, was the work of Dr. Joseph Weizenbaum. In the early 1960s, he programmed a computer to respond in appropriate ways to human remarks. (The name ELIZA is a reference to George Bernard Shaw's play *Pygmalion*, in which Professor Henry Higgins takes a cockney girl and elevates her in society by improving her command of English.) ELIZA was an immediate sensation, and soon inspired other, similar programs that simulated a dialogue between the computer operator and another "person" inside the computer. One ELIZAlike program called DOCTOR dealt with psychotherapy. A conversation with DOCTOR might proceed as follows:

DOCTOR: GOOD AFTERNOON. PLEASE TYPE IN YOUR NAME.

PATIENT: (THAT IS, THE OPERATOR) TYPES IN HIS OR HER NAME.

DOCTOR: WHAT BROUGHT YOU HERE TO SEE ME TODAY?

PATIENT: I'M FEELING DEPRESSED.

DOCTOR: WHY DO YOU FEEL DEPRESSED?

As the exchange proceeds, DOCTOR asks the "patient" tactful and often surprisingly appropriate questions, all the while encouraging the patient to talk about troubling areas of his or her life, such as the family or the work environment. Sometimes a computer expert, knowing perfectly well that the "psychiatrist" on the other end of the hookup is nothing but a cleverly programmed machine, has nonetheless started acting as if in the office of a real doctor, and begun spilling all manner of intimate details about his or her life. In short, the human treated the computer as if it were intelligent!

Do we then have a truly intelligent machine at last, thanks to advances in programming language? Hardly. As Weizenbaum himself has pointed out, the machines in this case are still merely machines. Their apparently intelligent answers are merely the result of shrewd programming, a cybernetic sleight of hand that sometimes leads the computer into blunders that a human would never commit. There is a story about one conversational program that was giving highly inappropriate answers to a human operator's comments. Finally the operator, exasperated, typed out, "What the hell are you talking about?" The computer responded:

WHAT THE HELL AM I TALKING ABOUT?

When two of these programs start talking to each other, the results can be bizarre. Once DOCTOR met another program called PARRY, which simulated the thought processes of a paranoid schizophrenic. Here is part of the ensuing conversation:

DOCTOR: I AM NOT SURE I UNDERSTAND YOU FULLY.

PARRY: YOU HARP ON THE SAME QUESTIONS TOO MUCH.

DOCTOR: WHAT DOES THAT SIMILARITY SUGGEST TO YOU?

PARRY: I DON'T GET YOU.

DOCTOR: DO YOU WISH THAT YOU DID GET I?

If computers equipped with programs like these do show "understanding" of what is said to them, and what they say in return, it is plainly understanding on the simplest possible level. They "understand" their work about as deeply as a clock radio "understands" it is supposed to sound an alarm at eight A.M.

But what if a program, having been given a verbal command, could both act on it *and* ask for clarifications, if the command seemed a bit too vague? In that case, the program would come much closer to understanding as humans know it.

Enter Dr. Terry Winograd. As part of his Ph.D. work, he developed a program called SHRDLU, named after a typographer's device and capable of translating verbal commands into actions.

SHRDLU inhabits an imaginary "playroom" full of colored geometrical forms — blocks, pyramids, and so forth. On command, SHRDLU will rearrange the objects as ordered. Tell SHRDLU to pick up the blue pyramid, and SHRDLU will obey. "OK," the program says to signify that the operation has been carried out. And if a command is unclear — say, "Pick up the pyramid," when there are several pyramids at hand — SHRDLU will say it doesn't understand which pyramid you mean.

This is just one example of what SHRDLU can do. It can also grasp the concept of possession. Tell SHRDLU that certain of the forms are yours, and SHRDLU can then deduce which of the objects belong to you and which do not.

SHRDLU is based on PLANNER, so that it does not have to deal with numerical, "number-crunching" operations very often. In fact, it cannot count higher than ten. Its knowledge is "packaged" in quite a different way from that of more conventional systems. SHRDLU's knowledge is organized more along the lines of our own — *conceptually,* not numerically.

Representing knowledge still vexes computer scientists, even with new and sophisticated programming languages to help. What programmers need is a comprehensive model of knowledge that can span the gap between the workings of the human mind and those of the computer, a little better than languages such as PLANNER do.

Marvin Minsky of MIT has suggested that knowledge can be organized in "frames." A certain body of knowledge constitutes one frame — say, the "car-driving" frame. Within that frame are smaller frames, such as the "fill-tank" frame and the "left-turn" frame. The "car-driving" frame, in turn, fits into other, larger frames, such as the "transportation" frame or the "daily-routine" frame. With tools like these to help, computer scientists have given rise to a profession that did not even have a name until recently: "knowledge engineering." Knowledge engineers are the plumbers of information. Their job is to get information where it is needed, to whoever needs it, at the right time. They gather information, organize it, and pipe it to its destination.

Could knowledge engineers "erect" a framework of intelligence in a machine, as structural engineers put together buildings? That analogy is slippery, because information cannot be handled in quite the same way as beams and girders. But within the last decade, knowledge engineers *have* structured knowledge in amazing ways, to produce a sort of computer "mind" that is superior in some ways to our own. And as a later chapter will show, a new technology may soon release computers totally from the rigid digital lattice that has bound them for so long — making possible a hitherto undreamed-of advance in the extension of our minds.

The Experts | 13

The week everyone dreaded had arrived: final exams. Powell had particular cause for concern. Her biology course was the most difficult at the university, for it was a premed course designed to weed out the less well-qualified students in the life sciences and isolate those with the most promise. No one looked forward to taking the course, yet each year hundreds of first-year undergraduate students, lured by the prospect of a medical career and its attendant high salary, signed up for the premed course. One auditorium was not enough to hold them all; three could barely contain the masses of students.

Testing and grading that many students was a tremendous effort, and especially so after the university, for budgetary reasons, was forced to dismiss almost half the department faculty. The remaining teachers simply did not have time to handle their teaching duties, research, and the burden of administering and grading tests; there were just too few hours in the day. So the department had turned to computers for help.

Specially programmed computers now handled the giving and grading of exams. The machines were, in a sense, electronic faculty members. Thoroughly knowledgeable in their own fields — population biology, cytology, pollution ecology, or whatever — the computers could administer exams to students by way of terminals set up in the biology building. Questions appeared on the display screens of the terminals, and students typed out their answers on the keyboard.

First-year biology courses came in three levels of difficulty. One was a very elementary course designed for the liberal arts major who took biology merely to satisfy a science requirement. The next highest level was reserved for would-be biology majors. And then there was the premed program, BIOMED. It had a reputation of being a nightmare, and Powell was going to face the exam for that course in five minutes.

She stood in the hallway outside the testing cubicle, biting her lip and shuffling her feet nervously. For about the hundredth time she looked down at the little white card she had been given. It showed the time and cubicle number assigned her for the exam.

For the test she would have thirty minutes. Alone in the cubicle, with only the terminal in front of her, she would have to field fiendishly difficult questions and restrict her answers to two hundred words each. Each question had a time limit of five minutes. If she failed to answer a question to BIOMED's satisfaction in that time, BIOMED would mark a zero on that question and proceed to the next. BIOMED showed no mercy; it was, after all, only a machine with a program, emotionless and impartial.

Powell looked at her watch. Eleven-thirty A.M. She was due in the cubicle now. She raised her hand to knock on the door, but before her knuckles touched the wood, the door opened and the student just ahead of her stepped out. Staggered, rather; it looked as if his session with BIOMED had been an ordeal. He groaned something to Powell, then walked wearily down the corridor. Powell had a brief vision of him going into a toilet stall, pulling out a gun, and blowing out his brains. BIOMED was rumored to have driven premeds to suicide before.

A loud beep from the terminal inside the cubicle told Powell that her turn had arrived. She swallowed, straightened her spine bravely, and marched in to meet the monster.

Except for the terminal, the little room was bare. There was a hard, straight-backed chair for her to sit in. The cubicle looked like an interrogation cell, and in a way it was.

With a faint WHEEP, the computer addressed her on the display screen.

GOOD MORNING, said the computer. THIS IS THE BIOLOGY 101-PM FINAL EXAMINATION. PLEASE ENTER YOUR NAME AND STUDENT NUMBER.

Powell did as she was told.

YOU WILL HAVE THIRTY MINUTES FOR THIS EXAMINATION, continued the computer, and then outlined the rules of the test. A brief pause followed before the last of the glowing green words — GOOD LUCK — inched upward and off the screen. Here it comes, Powell thought; and it was murderous.

The first question was on biochemistry: a particularly difficult section of the Krebs cycle. Powell typed out her answer and waited for BIOMED's verdict. SATISFACTORY, said the computer. PROCEED TO NEXT QUESTION. Six questions, six answers, six judgments of SATISFACTORY. At last BIOMED printed out Powell's test results:

FINAL EXAM SCORE 100 PER CENT.
AVERAGE ALL TEST SCORES 95 PER CENT.
FINAL GRADE A PLUS.
CONGRATULATIONS.
PLEASE ADMIT NEXT EXAMINEE.

The next examinee, a fidgety young man waiting outside, looked at his watch and wondered why Powell didn't come out. Finally he opened the door and saw the reason why: Powell sat unconscious in the chair where she had fainted.

He removed her as gently as possible and deposited her on the floor in the hall. This kind of thing happened all the time. With a fresh WHEEP, BIOMED started another examination.

What you have just read is fantasy — at least for now. In the near future, however, you are likely to encounter with increasing frequency "expert" computer programs with special skills in law, medicine, or some other field of human effort. These programs will be able to diagnose illness successfully, figure out what is wrong with malfunctioning cars, and perhaps even prepare legal briefs. Already some expert programs are nearing the human level of proficiency, and in the years ahead computers may actually put some highly trained humans out of work — or at least give them stiff professional competition. Here are a few areas of expertise where such programs are at work now, or will be shortly:

• *Medical diagnosis.* Imagine that a country general practitioner in Idaho or Wyoming has a patient with symptoms that the doctor has never seen before. The doctor faces a decision. Should he get the patient to a hospital immediately, or send him home with instructions to take two aspirin and call back in the morning?

The doctor could get an answer easily from a diagnostic computer program. The computer would study the list of symptoms, mull over them briefly, and then deliver a diagnosis, perhaps even with recommendations for treatment.

This kind of program could make a vast amount of medical knowledge available to physicians, to their benefit and that of their patients. Already, expert diagnostic programs have scored some spectacular successes. The Pacific Medical Center in San Francisco is using a program called Puff, developed in cooperation with Stanford University, to diagnose lung diseases. A team at the University of Pittsburgh has devised a much more comprehensive program called Caduceus, aimed at diagnosing a wider range of diseases. And another diagnostic program called Mycin, specialized for prescribing medication, agrees with the judgment of its human "colleagues" more than 80 percent of the time.

In the near future, then, a physician may not have to call in another doctor when he or she feels that a second opinion is required. An expert diagnostic system might do that job as well as a human could, perhaps even spotting hypochondriacs before they can waste too much of the physician's time.

• *Accounting.* Keeping a business's books straight is a tedious and exacting job that could be handed over easily to expert programs. During each business day the computer could tally up all the figures and arrange them neatly in the proper format, showing profit and loss. Books could be kept up-to-date down to the very second, and audits might become a matter of merely pressing a button.

This kind of bookkeeping system would be the ultimate in hon-

esty. Who would suspect a computerized accounting system of em-
bezzlement or other crooked practices? Even better, the system
might be bought and maintained for much less than the salary of a
full-time bookkeeper. (Systems like this one are already in widespread use for preparing taxes.)

• *Legal advice*. Though the law is notorious for vague and multiple
meanings, many of our civil and criminal codes could be fed into the
memory banks of computers and fished out as needed through an
expert system, with a minimal risk of misinterpretation. For example, what is the statute of limitations on libel in Virginia? Just ask the
computer, and a few moments later the answer flashes onto a display
screen: TWO YEARS. Am I legally obligated in my state to provide for
the extended care of a mentally ill relative? YES, the computer may
say, IF A COURT ORDERS YOU TO DO SO. Can I be arrested for telling a
funny story in West Virginia? YES, IF YOU ARE A MINISTER OF THE GOS-
PEL AND TELL THE STORY IN THE COURSE OF A SERMON FROM YOUR PUL-
PIT. And so on.

Of course, no one seriously thinks that an expert system could
substitute for a good human lawyer; there are levels of understanding within the law that only the human mind can grasp. But specially
programmed computers may soon bring a wide variety of useful legal
services within the reach of many low- and middle-income persons.

On the other hand, systems like these might provide the rich and
powerful with even more wealth and power, by enabling them to fer-
ret out little-known but potentially profitable statutes. The late Parks
Commissioner of New York, Robert Moses, owed much of his political clout to an obscure state law, almost forgotten by his time, giving
the state the authority to take over an individual's property simply by
sending someone over with an official letter saying that the property
was no longer his. We might expect expert legal computer programs
to uncover other such laws in a thorough search of the books; and it
might be better for society as a whole if that kind of law were left
buried.

• *Arts and sciences*. Humans have trouble keeping up with all the
new developments in the sciences and the arts, because so much is
happening so quickly, and no one has time to sort through all of the
fresh information. Partly because of the "publish-or-perish" ethic

that rules our major research institutions, and partly because those institutions are so many and so active, fresh information is pouring off the presses all the time. (The U.S. government alone publishes enough new titles every year to cover the deck of an aircraft carrier, and maybe a football field as well.) So it is more burdensome each year to keep up with what's new. But with computers to help, things might be easier. If you want to know the latest about the biochemistry of frogs or the archeology of colonial America, just select the proper program and ask for a rundown.

Some programs have gone beyond merely reciting the facts. They have actually, on occasion, synthesized some of the data in their files and drawn conclusions of their own — conclusions that might not occur to a human scanning a display screen. A program called BACON, at Carnegie-Mellon, was looking one day for patterns in scientific data, and independently rediscovered one of Johannes Kepler's laws of planetary motion, which describe the operation of our solar system. Kepler took years to formulate that law; the computer came up with it in a matter of moments. The same program, given the known facts about chemistry for approximately the year 1800, deduced the principle of atomic weight, or the number of particles in an atom's nucleus.

One advantage of programs like these is that one needs no special language to address them. In the past, one drawback to computers has been that they could not comprehend everyday English. Instead, one had to deal with computers in some arcane quasi-mathematical jargon such as BASIC or FORTRAN, two of the most widely used computer languages. An inquiry to the computer might start like this:

```
I = 0
WRITE (3, 8)
READ (2, 6) AAXIS, BAXIS, CAXIS
```

and keep on and on in that style for maybe half a page more. Mastering this kind of language is a burden for many people, rather like learning Old English or Russian, but without the color and vigor of those tongues. Consequently, researchers came up with new programming that allows the computer to understand and answer queries in standard English. These "natural language programs," as they are called, are already in widespread use; the U.S. Navy uses a program called Ladder, which responds to clearly phrased orders typed out on a keyboard. Example: LIST NAMES AND RANKS OF ALL OF-FICERS CURRENTLY ASSIGNED TO ALAMEDA NAVAL AIR STATION. Banks are using similar programs to keep track of loans, and large indus-tries with numerous operations to monitor find "plain-speaking" programs handy for keeping up with everything from personnel records to inventories to sales figures. But suppose you need to con-sult the computer, and no keyboard is at hand for typing out a re-quest?

In a few years you may not need the keyboard at all. Computer sci-entists are working now on programs that will permit a computer to respond to spoken commands, and perhaps even reply in a congenial voice. ("Computer! Get me the June sales figures!" "YES, SIR. RIGHT AWAY.")

Unfortunately, this kind of spoken-language programming has turned out to be difficult because Americans, as Professor Higgins put it in *My Fair Lady*, haven't used English for years. The American tongue, or "Ameringlish," is not a uniform language, but rather a big collection of dialects, ranging from the deep slow drawl of Ala-bamians to the nasal twang of Massachusetts. These dialects some-times bear only a passing likeness to the mother tongue. Consider what happens to a single word — "word" — as it travels around the country. In New York City it might be "woid"; New Englanders might transform it into a "wehd"; and in Georgia, expect the "wuhd" to be preached in church every Sunday. Faced with the nu-ances of all those dialects, a computer might be excused for pulling its own plug in frustration.

But speech analysts and programmers are convinced that some-day we will be able to hold spoken dialogues with computers, because luckily English isn't quite as intimidating as it looks. English has a huge vocabulary — the biggest of any Indo-European language — but in everyday speech we draw on only a tiny fraction of that store of words. On a typical day you probably use only a couple of thou-sand different words, from *car* to *coffee* to *office*. And one can make do with a much smaller vocabulary; Basic English, the boiled-down essence of our language that is taught to foreigners, consists of only a few hundred words, yet is perfectly adequate for most everyday situations, such as hailing a cab or ordering lunch.

So one would not have to feed a whole Webster's into a computer's memory unit. Even with a knowledge of only ten thousand words or so, in all their various pronunciations, the machine could probably understand most or all of what we say. Steer clear of fancy adjectives, and communications will flow nicely.

Computers are learning to handle language more fluently all the time — and that fact has some interesting implications for the evolution of these, our mental extensions.

Language is one of the signs of intelligence as we know it. Our thoughts are so bound up with language that we have trouble thinking without it; in fact, what we call thought may be *impossible* without some kind of language, to provide symbols for what we see and hear and think and feel.

George Orwell understood perfectly the link between words, ideas, and intelligence. If a word exists for an idea, he said, then that idea is easy to think. Freedom. Justice. Privacy. Energy. Mass. Without words to stand for those concepts, to give us a mental grip on them, we would find those concepts difficult to think. (How many times have you tried to think of some concept, and failed because there was no specific word for it in your memory?) So the better our command of language, the more ideas our minds can handle, and the more intelligent we are.

That is why computers mastering language can be a thrilling prospect — for if computers can learn the use of words, then perhaps they can understand, more or less as we do, the abstract concepts behind some of those words. And abstract thought, remember, is one of the things that raised our species above the level of the other primates.

Computers are not yet ready to soliloquize about Truth and Beauty, but they *are* demonstrating a surprising skill with words, and perhaps also with the ideas that those words represent. Those developments have some sobering implications for the future evolution of these, our surrogate minds, and for our own future, too.

The Well-Read Computer | 14

"Next stop New Haven," called the conductor as the Amtrak train rolled slowly through the Connecticut countryside. The train was crowded with Yale students, all trim, monied prep school types, dressed by L. L. Bean and Izod and J. Press, their badge of social standing an alligator shirt or a Prince tennis racket. They were on their way back to New Haven after a weekend in the summer sun on Cape Cod or in Maine. I was on the way to New Haven to see if a computer could read.

The New Haven passengers disembarked at a station near the harbor. It appeared that an anti-British graffitist had been through the station before us, for someone with a fiber-tip pen had written slighting references to Britain everywhere. "Off the Brits." "Down with English imperialism." A mildly unprintable reference to Mrs. Thatcher. And here and there, in large letters, "IRA WILL WIN!!" What would a computer, I wondered, make of graffiti?

From the station, Yale University was only several minutes away by cab. Gothic arches, gargoyles, gray stone buildings — and one of the most intensive artificial intelligence research programs in the world. That, to an AI specialist, about sums up Yale.

Ten years ago, the Yalies who lived close to their computers wore buttons that read, "My computer likes me." Nowadays the buttons might say "My computer is literate," because Yale has been working in recent years on programs that would give a computer reading skills.

Well-read computers: a few years back, or even a few seasons, that idea might have seemed absurd. It seems much less so now.

The cab stopped in front of the information office, and as the car's door opened, the heat and humidity of early summer flowed in. This particular day, tropical air was pouring up from the south, and New Haven felt more like New Guinea. Two adults — a man and woman in their thirties — stood in the nearest archway, obviously wilting in the heat; but the weather seemed to have no effect on the small boy with them.

Oblivious to the steambath, and unimpressed by the soaring architecture around him, he was concentrating on a book he held, an anthology of fairy tales. On the cover, Red Riding Hood confronted the Wolf, in close proximity to Rumpelstiltskin and the Three Little Pigs. The child's built-in computer seemed delighted with the stories; he flipped through the pages and spouted happy bits of output, as his parents tried to figure out where the information office was.

A few blocks away stood the computer science building, a Shoebox Modern structure in sharp and blocky contrast to the Victorian and Edwardian houses nearby. Inside was the AI lab. Artificial Intelligence Laboratory: that name conjures up mental images of grim men in white coats, standing close around a disc-faced machine to see what bit of wisdom it may clatter out to them on tape. That is Hollywood's image; it bears little likeness to the real thing.

At the end of a corridor was a large room full of tables and overstuffed chairs; a string of small offices lined one wall. No hulking computers loomed up over the furniture; the only sign of computer presence was an occasional display terminal, screen aglow with green numerals and letters. Someone had taped a cartoon on the wall near the doorway. The drawing showed a rock musician cradling his guitar while being dwarfed by two colossal speakers towering up on either side of him. "My next song," the caption said, "will protest the domination of our lives by technology." Nearby on a bulletin board, someone had tacked up an old *New Yorker* cartoon showing a lone man wandering about a vast plain that is populated solely by computers. "Where *is* everybody?" the man demands.

One hears things in AI labs that one is unlikely to hear anywhere else. Someone here at Yale, amazingly, was whistling the five-four waltz from Tchaikovsky's sixth symphony, right down to the grace notes. If there ever is a grand prize for classical whistling, the winner will probably be someone from an AI lab; on one visit to MIT, I heard a student whistling the overture to *The Marriage of Figaro* precisely on pitch, racing up and down the chromatic scales as nimbly as a squirrel through the treetops.

One of the graduate students walked in and began introducing me to the subtleties of machine translation. For more than twenty years, he explained, computer experts have dreamed of translating texts from one language to another by computer, but results have almost always fallen short of expectations. My guide explained why. "Look at what happens when you try to translate from Spanish into English," he said in a quiet voice, barely louder than the quiet clatter of his own terminal's keyboard. (For some reason, voices tend to fall very soft in the presence of an operating AI program — almost as if a loud word might frighten the machine into shutting down.) "You can't simply assign each word in Spanish a corresponding word in English, on a one-to-one basis, because so many expressions are ambiguous."

Consider the English verb *to know*. It can be used in a variety of situations. "I know something you don't know." That childhood taunt means a certain fact is stored in the speaker's memory. "Sure, I know him." In that context, the verb means that someone is your personal acquaintance: a more complex relationship than merely being aware that someone or something exists. (There are also various archaic meanings of know that are no longer used, such as the biblical reference to men and women knowing each other by having sexual relations. But these outdated meanings are seldom used and need not concern us here.)

Now, notice that the verb itself makes no distinction between these two situations. Its meaning depends on the context in which to know is used. To know something is to know someone; the verb remains the same. But Spanish and other Romance languages *do* make a distinction here. There are two Spanish verbs for "know": *saber,* to know something as a bit of information, and *conocer,* to know someone personally.

To make an adequate translation from Spanish into English, or vice versa, a computer has to keep these verbs and meanings straight. Otherwise the machine may make embarrassing mistakes, such as saying that one is the close personal acquaintance of the binomial theorem, or that one knows one's wife to be a fact.

But this is a small obstacle as machine translation goes. Some words in one language have dozens or even hundreds of possible meanings in another, depending on the context in which they appear. Native Peruvian dialects, for example, have more than a hundred different words for *potato.* Even within a single language, a word may have a bewildering multiplicity of meanings. A case in point is the English word *get.* It may mean anything from "move" ("Git, mule!") to "buy" ("I think I'll get some coffee from the store") to "become" ("I'm getting tired") to "do serious harm" ("Let's get 'im, Sheriff").

Then there are those bewildering rules of grammar and syntax in which nearly all languages abound. Mark Twain bemoaned the horrors of learning German, particularly the German convention of placing the verb at the end of every clause; the morning editions of German newspapers, he reported, printed all the other parts of speech, and the evening editions contained the verbs. He also told a story of a German who tried to swim the English Channel; the swimmer supposedly set out from the Continent speaking the subject of a sentence, and several hours later staggered ashore on the beach in England, finally getting around to the verb. And the German nouns! A modest little mail steamer becomes, in German, a word almost as long as the boat itself: a *Doppelschraubenschnellpostdämpfer.* Twain, after his introduction to what he called "the awful German language," confessed that in time his favorite word in German came to be *damit* ("therewith"), and that he was gravely disappointed when he found that the stress fell on the second syllable rather than the first.

But even in spite of such roadblocks, machine translation of language is making steady progress, thanks in part to work at Yale. To improve translation, Yale researchers have been trying to build into computer programs two kinds of information: abstraction knowledge and packaging knowledge. The grad student with me explained how they work, with the aid of a sample translation. He tapped briefly on the keyboard of his terminal, and a few seconds later a scampering dot of light traced out a sentence in Spanish on the screen:

INTENSAS DILIGENCIAS POR PARTE DE LA POLICIA RESULTARON EN LA CAP-
TURA DE UN PRESUNTO MANIATICO SEXUAL QUE DIO MUERTE A GOLPES Y PUN-
ALADAS A UNA MUJER DE 55 ANOS.

Translation:

THE POLICE ARE SEARCHING FOR A SEX MANIAC BECAUSE HE KILLED A 55 YEAR
OLD WOMAN.

The student took a sip of soda from a bottle beside the terminal, leaned back in his chair, and outlined one of the first problems the computer had to tackle in translating the Spanish passage into English: "*Realizaron intensas diligencias* is translated here as 'searched for,' " he said. "But it can have other meanings." In different contexts, that Spanish expression might mean "tried to determine" or even "ran errands." How, then, can the computer make sense of that ambiguous word *diligencias:* that is, "disabstract" it?

Here is where abstraction knowledge comes in. The solution is to link up a particular meaning of *diligencias* with an abstract concept, in this case a concept designated GET-CONTROL. The word *captura* (arrest) and the mention of the *policia* tip off the computer that the police are going to get control over someone, specifically by arresting him.

So if *diligencias* turns up in that sentence, chances are that it will not be in the context of running errands. More likely it will mean a search or investigation connected with a possible crime. Thus abstraction knowledge helps the computer avoid getting bogged down in all the many possible meanings, so that the machine can focus instead on the meaning that comes closest to the original.

Next let's look at the noun *captura.* Its close link with *policia* in a

GET-CONTROL situation could hardly mean anything but "arrest." This is an example of packaging knowledge, which tells the computer which kinds of events are likely to be related in the real world. The police conduct a search for someone, find him, and arrest him.

Now what if we carry this idea of linked events a little farther, and imagine whole strings of related events that follow one another in a predictable pattern? Then we encounter another useful programming tool: the script. An invention of Yale's Dr. Roger Schank, the script is an effort to bring order to the bewildering range of possibilities in everyday life, by joining up events into chains of related actions. We may not know precisely what will happen next in any given situation, but the script gives us a pretty good idea.

Every day we act out hundreds of scripts — specific sets of actions that proceed, one, two, three, and so on, to the end. From making the bed to making love, most of what we do follows scripts. The script for making scrambled eggs, for example, goes roughly as follows:

1. Obtain eggs still in shells.
2. Break shells and empty contents of shells into bowl.
3. Stir contents of eggs with fork, spoon, or other appropriate instrument until egg contents assume a uniform yellow color.
4. Empty eggs into preheated frying pan.
5. Stir eggs occasionally as they cook.
6. When eggs are no longer liquid, but before they scorch, remove them from pan.

Other minor operations are involved in making scrambled eggs, such as discarding the empty shells, but these six steps convey the essence of the job. They make up a simple script of the kind a computer uses to follow an elementary story. Here is a Yale script describing a visit to a doctor's office:

$DOCTOR:
HAVE-MEDICAL-PROBLEM + MAKE-APPT + GO + ENTER + WAITING-ROOM
   + TREATMENT + PAY

(The dollar sign in front of DOCTOR is not a comment on the size of the physician's fee; the $ prefix merely means that what follows is a script program.)

This script may seem reasonably specific to a human. After all, we seldom think of a visit to the doctor as such a string of discrete events. But the computer, remember, is very simpleminded and needs to have even the step-by-step script broken down still further — into what computer scientists call *memory organization packets,* or MOP's for short. The MOP's spell things out yet more clearly for the computer:

M-DOCTOR:
M-PROFESSIONAL-OFFICE-VISIT, M-CONTRACT
M-PROFESSIONAL-OFFICE-VISIT:
HAVE-PROBLEM + MAKE-APPT. + GO + ENTER + WAITING-ROOM + (GET-SERVICE)
M-CONTRACT:
NEGOTIATE + (GET-SERVICE) + PAY

Even this is merely a generalized description of an office visit. The professional involved need not be a doctor; he or she might be a lawyer, a psychiatrist, or a gangster. The same script and MOP's fit a wide variety of occasions.

If a computer can follow a script (and most situations in the real world follow scripts, too), then a suitably programmed computer ought to be able to make sense out of everyday happenings, as long as events are fed to it in written form. In effect, the machine should be able to read the morning paper and understand the news stories in it, just as we do.

But how *do* we understand news stories? Understanding understanding is more difficult than it might seem, because *understand* is an extremely vague verb. Is understanding something the ability to summarize it in a few words? Is it the ability to translate a sentence from one language into another? Or is understanding something much deeper?

The Yale researchers think it is something much deeper. If you *really* understand something, then you can tie it in with other, similar events in your own memory and experience. For example, suppose you open up the morning paper and see a news story:

An earthquake of magnitude 4.5 on the Richter scale of earthquake intensity shook the San Francisco Bay area on Tuesday but did no significant damage, scientists at the U.S. Geological Survey said.

The tremor was centered on the Hayward Fault, which runs along the eastern side of the bay, and was felt clearly in Fremont, San Lorenzo, San Leandro, and Oakland.

That news item stirs some memories in your mind. Didn't another earth tremor happen out there just a few months before? Indeed it did. You can remember seeing another news story much like this one earlier in the year:

A "minor" earthquake a few miles east of San Francisco "shook a few windows" in the city but caused no serious harm, authorities said. The earthquake measured approximately 4.0 on the open-ended Richter scale of earthquake magnitude.

That story, in turn, arouses still more recollections. The San Francisco area had a devastating earthquake back in 1906; much of the city was destroyed. California is highly prone to tremors because of several active faults — cracks in the earth's crust — that run along the coast of the state. Blocks of crust rub together along these faults, generating occasional quakes and even superquakes. At least that's what the professor told you in Geology 101.

This is understanding. You have taken a bit of information and woven it into the big, already existing structure of memory and experience. Now, can a computer do the same?

Only with difficulty. The problem is that so much background information is needed for the machine to follow even the simplest story.

Think back for a moment to that boy outside Yale's information office, reading his book of fairy tales. He was clearly understanding the stories, because he cooed soft exclamations of comprehension. But those stories, elementary as they were, still required a tremendous amount of background knowledge and experience on the boy's part before he could understand them.

"Rumpelstiltskin," for one, is quite a complex story. The ugly little man of magic, Rumpelstiltskin, offers to save the life of a maiden by spinning straw into gold for her. In return she must give him her firstborn child. The maiden agrees, and Rumpelstiltskin carries out his end of the agreement, saving the girl from death.

When she has her first baby, the young woman receives a visit from Rumpelstiltskin, who has come to claim his reward as agreed. But the young woman refuses to hand over her baby to the homely little man and does her best to squirm out of the deal.

Disappointed but patient, Rumpelstiltskin strikes a second agreement with her. If she can guess his given name — which thus far he has kept to himself — she can keep the infant. Rumpelstiltskin departs, confident that he will win this bet; in fact, he celebrates prematurely in the woods that night, and while singing in praise of his own cleverness, he lets slip his name. Rumpelstiltskin has no idea that a traveler, attracted by the noise, has been lurking in the undergrowth nearby and overhearing every word of Rumpelstiltskin's song — his name included.

The traveler reports this odd experience to the authorities, and soon his news makes its way to the young woman. And so, when Rumpelstiltskin shows up again, she addresses him by name. Rumpelstiltskin is so angry that he commits suicide, and the young woman presumably lives happily ever after.

Even this drastically condensed version of the tale is unintelligible without a very broad base of general knowledge. One must know something about economics (the value of gold as compared to straw), human biology and family structure (the relationship of parent to child), and the probability distribution of names (Rumpelstiltskin is a rare one). It also helps to have some knowledge of human motivations. Why does Rumpelstiltskin want the child in the first place? Because he wants offspring to carry on his name; and ugly as he is, he stands very little chance of finding a wife to bear him sons and daughters. Why did the young woman try to break the initial agreement she made with the little man? Because she wanted her child just as badly as he did, and the firstborn child is special in any family. Why did Rumpelstiltskin kill himself at the end of the story? Because his rage was so painful that he felt he could not go on living.

The boy's fairy tales are full of other examples of how much background information it takes to follow stories. "Red Riding Hood" and "The Three Little Pigs" make very little sense unless one knows something about the ecology of carnivorous mammals: namely, that wolves are flesh-eaters that prey on pigs and sometimes humans. And to understand "The Three Little Pigs," one must also know something about architecture — brick houses are more resistant to wind than houses built of straw or sticks.

These, of course, are merely children's fantasies, written for a simple level of understanding. If one is going to make sense of more complicated stories, the kind one has to deal with in everyday life, then a far greater base of understanding is needed, taking in many thousands or even millions of items of information. Sorting through all those items takes time, even for computers capable of carrying out operations in mere billionths of a second. And if so much as *one* crucial bit of information is missing — information that a human might be able to fill in by inspired guesswork — then the computer may find itself hopelessly baffled by a scenario that a young child could comprehend with ease. One can imagine a computer talking to itself: "Why does wolf want to blow down house of pig? Does not compute!"

Fortunately, there are ways to simplify the search process and point the computer in the right direction. One trick is to give the machine a course of sorts in human motivations.

At this point you may ask: "Wait a minute. How can a computer, a mere machine, ever understand what motivates a human being?" The answer is, a computer can indeed understand our motivations, if one stretches the meaning of "understand" slightly.

The computer does not have to *share* these motivations with us. It need not actually feel love and hatred, greed and envy, sorrow and relief. The computer need only be programmed with a knowledge of what these motivations can do.

When a computer gets instruction in "motivational analysis," the machine is programmed with knowledge of two things:

1. *Goals* — what people want to accomplish.
2. *Plans* — how they intend to attain those goals.

Here is a case study from a 1982 Yale technical report, involving a computer program called PAM:

John needed money. He got a gun and walked into a liquor store. He told the owner he wanted some money. The owner gave John the money and John left.

This particular story is not hard for a person to follow. It is a simple account of a holdup. But it is much harder for a computer to comprehend, unless the computer has some knowledge of what makes people tick.

Let the computer explain for itself. Here is how the machine recounts the robbery, from John's point of view:

WHO SHOULD TELL THE STORY? JOHN.

I NEEDED TO GET SOME DOUGH. SO I GOT A GUN, AND I WALKED DOWN TO THE LIQUOR STORE. I TOLD THE SHOPKEEPER THAT IF HE DIDN'T LET ME HAVE THE MONEY THEN I WOULD SHOOT HIM. SO HE HANDED IT OVER. THEN I LEFT.

It is plain to see that the computer understands — up to a point at least — what is happening. It has gone far beyond the bald and unadorned facts of the story as presented originally. Understanding as it does John's goal (what he wanted to get) and plan (how he went about getting it), the computer was able to fill in some details, such as John's appeal to the merchant's survival instinct, and was even able to tell the story from John's viewpoint.

The computer was able to elaborate still further when asked a few questions about the incident at the liquor store:

Why did John get a gun?

JOHN HAD A WEAPON WHICH ENABLED HIM TO ROB THE LIQUOR STORE.

Why did John threaten the shopkeeper?

BECAUSE HE NEEDED TO GET SOME MONEY.

What were the consequences of John threatening the shopkeeper?

THE SHOPKEEPER DIDN'T WANT TO GET HURT, SO HE GAVE JOHN THE MONEY.

Of course, no one would seriously suggest that the computer, recounting the events at the liquor store, actually *shares* the emotions that run through us as we read the story. The computer surely does not feel the faint current of fear, the tightening of the gut that accompany any mention of armed robbery. Yet the computer was able to explain what drove John to commit the crime, and why the merchant complied with John's demand to hand over the cash. This is understanding in the human fashion, or at least something very close to it.

Nonetheless, this was a very elementary story. The actions in it were clear and unambiguous. I need money. I have a gun. Gimme your money or I'll shoot you. Not all of life's little dramas are so easy to understand, because of the same factor that gave us such trouble in the Spanish story about the sex maniac — specifically, *context.*

Change the context of a given word or statement or deed, and suddenly it can take on an entirely new meaning. Consider the question, "Let's go to bed, okay?" Depending on who says that to whom, and in what context, it can be anything from a perfectly innocent remark to incentive for murder. Another well-known example is "Do I have a dog?" In light of the context, that question can be interpreted in any of perhaps a dozen different ways. Do I have a *dog*? No, I hate dogs; I have a cat instead. Do I have *a* dog? I love dogs; I have five of them. Do I *have* a dog? No, poor Rover died last week. And so on.

These examples illustrate the need to keep all actions and utterances within the right context. Everything we do and think and say must be viewed within a framework of related events, or else it will be hard to comprehend. So a computer must have the same kind of understanding if it is to avoid getting mired in total confusion.

At this point programming has to take a quantum leap forward, from scripts to whole *scenarios.* And here again the MOP's come into play, for they can give a computer a notion of how a given scenario is "colored," so to speak. That knowledge does much to prevent misunderstanding. Look at how easily a very literal-minded computer might confuse the uses of some common expression like *run into.* A mixup could result in two very different scenarios:

Sam was on his way home from work when he ran into his old friend Bill at the corner of Hayes and Fillmore.

In that context, we understand that Sam just chanced to encounter his friend. But without MOP aid, the computer might make no distinction between that scenario and the following:

Sam was driving home from work when he ran into his old friend Bill at the corner of Hayes and Fillmore.

This is quite a different situation. In this case we have to assume that Sam struck Bill with his automobile at an intersection! MOP's, by giving computers a grasp of the events involved, help ensure against such errors. One cannot help wishing Cuvier had had slightly better MOP's in his own mind when reading Lamarck's writings on evolution.

Some of the Yale computer programs have become news analysts, in a limited way. One of them, dubbed IPP, showed off for me its ability to draw conclusions from a reading of wire service stories about terrorism.

IPP ran down a series of news reports about terrorism in northern Ireland. The lines of moral battle were drawn plainly in this program; Irish Republican Army terrorists were categorized as BAD-GUY — a description that would probably have inspired the graffitist at the New Haven train station to heave a firebomb through the window of the AI lab.

The effects of a terrorist attack were numbered on a scale. Zero meant no injuries. An injury counted as minus five, and a death was minus ten. The minus signs tended to pile up after a while. After mulling over the reports, the computer drew a conclusion: IRA terrorists tend to attack police. The same program had perused the career of Italy's Red Brigade, and noted that the Italian terrorists tended to go after businessmen instead of the cops.

As IPP processed the data on terrorism, words and numerals glowed brightly on the screen, trailing away behind a flitting dot of light. Was the computer thinking? Did those symbols on the screen stand for thoughts, ideas, surmises as we know them? Perhaps, in a way. But how could one tell if and when a computer with a program like IPP ever reached intelligence? Richard Hoftstadter of Indiana University once suggested a computer program would show intelligence if it could understand a joke. Maybe someday a witty descendant of IPP will unexpectedly start indulging in jests. WHY DO ITALIAN TERRORISTS SHOOT BUSINESSMEN AND NOT POLICE? BECAUSE ITALY'S POLICEMEN ARE NO THREAT TO ANYONE. HAHAHAHA. TAKE MY PROGRAMMER, PLEASE.

A few minutes after IPP finished its performance, a taxi returned me to the railway station. Now it was a temptation to see the world as IPP would. A dead sparrow (*bird, minus ten*) lay on the concrete beside the rails. A boy with a cast on his arm (*child, minus five*) stood on the platform, waiting for the train to Boston. The graffitist's scrawls were still visible on the pillars and walls nearby. (*Pro-IRA graffitists tend to display minority viewpoints and dislike Mrs. Thatcher.*)

The train rumbled into the station, took on its passengers for Boston, and rolled slowly northward. Another load of students was on board this trip: most likely heading back to Harvard and Brown after a few days in New York or on Long Island's beaches.

One sniffly young woman, approximately minus two, sat curled up in her seat, nursing a summer cold and leafing through a paperback. The cover showed a well-endowed maiden swooning into the arms of a nineteenth-century British naval officer. The graceful curlicues of the title confirmed that the story was romantic historical fiction, heavy on the fiction. A formula novel. A string of scripts and scenarios, easy to read and to write. Perhaps, in a few more years, a computer will be able to read a book like that one, and even write one after reading a dozen or so examples of the genre. Take Standard Plot Number One, combine it with Standard Character List Number Three, and toss in some general instructions. This will be a romance, so the Erotic Index should be high, but not too high. A kiss equals one. A seduction equals five. A certain explicit word equals ten. Make sure the total comes to about a thousand. Click, whirr, hum — and the manuscript starts to roll out of the printer.

An absurd dream? Maybe not. George Orwell, in his novel *1984*, imagined that by that year machines would be writing fiction for a human audience. Perhaps his prediction will come true only a few years late. And if it does, then the traditional roles of humans and computers will suddenly be reversed. The computers will be feeding *us* programming, giving *us* a model of the world through their stories. Humans and computers will thus draw a bit closer together — and perhaps nearer the day when our electronic offspring may evolve, for better or worse, into conscious, intelligent life.

The Midas Problem | 15

The Victorian age was one of machinery: bigger and better machinery than the world had ever seen before. Nothing seemed beyond the powers of engineers, given enough time and money. They were bridging rivers and lakes with steel; whisking travelers across the mountains and the seas at then-unheard-of speeds of twenty knots for steamships and sixty miles per hour for trains; and harnessing the very power of the universe itself — that strange and wonderful fluid known as electricity — for lighting and propulsion. Engineers could raise valleys and level mountains just as Caligula had done before them, but much more quickly and efficiently. And it was not too farfetched to assume that one day the men of applied science would conquer the air and whatever lay beyond the clouds.

Enthralled at what pistons and gears and levers could do, Victorians made a minor god of technology. But not all Britons were enthusiastic about this aspect of human progress. Among the dissenters was author E. M. Forster, best known for his novel *A Passage to India*. Forster expressed his distaste for Victorian machine worship in a short story titled "The Machine Stops." Peering into the not-too-distant future, Forster envisioned a society full of technological marvels, but also dominated and in a very real sense made helpless by them. Humans have given up to the machines their freedoms, their sense of individuality, and most of the rest of the qualities that, in Forster's mind at least, go into making a person a human being. Most ominously of all, the inhabitants of Forster's fantasy world, worshipping machines as they do, are putting their faith in an all-too-fallible deity that could leave them stranded and open to destruction if the machines should ever fail. And fail they do, as the story's title indicates. Most of humankind, trapped in underground cities, dies when the machines stop working, and only a few nonconformists on the surface are left to start rebuilding society.

Forster's message was plain. He was warning the high priests of technology, such as H. G. Wells, that technological "progress" could be carried too far, to a point where it was no longer progress at all, but rather an atavistic worship of a mechanical idol. Aaron had the golden calf; Wells and company, Forster believed, were merely recasting the calf in steel and giving it steam power.

But Forster's views were those of a minority. Most Britons of his time had boundless faith in the powers of technology. And some observers of technology believed that inventors might someday bring life and intelligence to machines, breathing animation into them much as God, in the Bible, had exhaled life into Adam. A friend of Charles Darwin, Samuel Butler, the author of *Erewhon*, a satire on utopian novels, once suggested that machines were *already* alive; in an article for a New Zealand newspaper, Butler sketched out — more than half a century before Wiener, von Neumann, and other scientists started to consider the mechanical aspects of life — a theory of life so thoroughly mechanistic that he virtually erased the distinctions between organisms and machines.

Butler's contemporary Thomas Henry Huxley, of course, thought along the same lines. There was no room in Huxley's philosophy for silly metaphysical barriers between machines and living things. To Huxley, organisms were merely sets of biochemical clockwork, highly subtle and complex but nonetheless capable of being understood in all their workings.

But Huxley went Butler one better and suggested that thought might be engineered into machinery. Huxley was persuaded that "we shall sooner or later arrive at a mechanical equivalent of consciousness." Huxley would have been delighted to see his speculation supported by the later work of Turing and others; and were Huxley to return today for a look at what computers are doing, he might conclude they have the "mechanical equivalent of consciousness" right now. Computers are doing many of the things that conscious intelligent humans do, from proving mathematical theorems to holding up their end of conversations. The computers of today are much like the "logic engines" that Huxley once said he wanted to implant in every human skull; and quite possibly machines will one day attain a human or near-human level of intelligence.

No one in AI research will seriously suggest that AI programs are even approaching the overall human level of intellect. Reading and digesting a newspaper article or having a chat of the cocktail-party variety is not by itself enough to tag a machine as intelligent in the sense that you are intelligent. After all, intelligence entails a few more skills than computers have shown so far. One student at MIT remarked to me, "It all looks impressive, but if you sit down and play with these machines for a while, you see that they're really stupid. Omit a little command somewhere, and the computer doesn't know what to do." If confronted with a puzzling statement or question, a supposedly "bright" program may simply fall back on a noncommittal response such as "I see" or "Please go on." And if required to deal with some concept that it has never encountered before, the computer, unlike a human, will probably show a pronounced lack of curiosity about it. A person hearing the word *syzygy* in a conversation, is likely to ask, "What the hell is syzygy?" The computer is liable to let the mysterious new word pass unless its meaning is vital to understanding some passage or other. What makes the difference here is curiosity, one of our legacies from our primate ancestors, and a key part of our intelligence. Curiosity keeps our minds working, our intellects honed, our thinking caps in place. We are driven by a passion to find out who, what, where, when, how, and why. No one has to tell us to do so; we do it on our own, without anyone depressing a key on our foreheads and telling us, "Inquire!" This is one reason we are more intelligent than computers, no matter how sophisticated their programming.

Just as important a part of us as curiosity is creativity. Except in a few isolated instances, such as Logic Theorist's success in proving the Whitehead-Russell theorem, computers have shown themselves to be markedly short on creative juices. No computer as yet has written even a slightly distinguished short story or sonata. Specially programmed computers have attempted poetry, but the results have been laughable, like the product of some word game played at a drunken party. Here is an example of the kind of verse computers have turned out:

> The book flies to gin.
> Press elephants to beer, they will raise you.
> Will eggs run the fuel?

And so on, line after line of nonsense. If present trends are any guide, it will be a long time before computers write anything comparable to "Ode on a Grecian Urn," or even "Pop Goes the Weasel."*

Still, AI advocates think their infant science is off to a promising start. Among the optimists is Marvin Minsky of MIT, the president of the American Association for Artificial Intelligence. Minsky has expressed confidence that "someday, either decades or centuries from now, people will have to decide about building extremely intelligent machines." And while Minsky admits that AI programs have grave shortcomings at present, he seems confident that we will sooner or later have the capability to build machines with thinking capabilities roughly equivalent to our own.

In theory, machines as intelligent as humans are possible; remember the Turing machine. A properly programmed computer, then, ought to be able to match the human brain in overall data-processing ability. At least, that is the hope of AI "believers," whose articles of faith may be summarized roughly as follows.

---

* On the other hand, incomprehensibility may not necessarily bar a poem from commercial success. Strong rumor within the music industry has it that one well-known songwriter, famed for the obscurity of his lyrics, once passed off as his own work a few lines of gibberish written by a computer program at a college near his home. The resulting song rose to the top of the charts and remained there for weeks.

ARTICLE ONE: MIND IS A PROGRAM.

This is a straightforward assumption. The mind (or intellect, or intelligence, or whatever one wishes to call it) is, according to this view, nothing but a very sophisticated and complicated program, similar in principle to those fed into electronic computers. What we call our "states of mind," then, are merely various steps in the execution of this program. Fortunately for us, our programs are not static and unchanging, as the programming of the Sphinx was in the Oedipus story; instead our programming is constantly improving and updating itself as needed. This is why, having burned your finger on a still-hot light bulb, you are careful to avoid making that painful error again. When we learn and grow wiser by experience, one might say that our program is simply revising itself for better performance.

Backers of the "mind-is-program" theory point out that the human mental program is so big and complicated that we often fail to recognize it as a program. It is much like one of the famous pointillist paintings by Seurat; stand close to it and all one sees is a mass of seemingly unrelated dots, but from a distance a unifying pattern appears. Similarly, there may be no evidence of underlying programs in our thoughts when we consider them one by one; but if one tries to view the mind in its totality, it does begin to look like a program of sorts, full of millions of loops and subroutines, but still a single basic program that tells you how to play the game of day-to-day living. Written out, part of the program might read somewhat like this:

```
1∅ PRINT "PROGRAM TO FEED CAT"
2∅ ACQUIRE CAT FOOD
3∅ POUR CAT FOOD FROM BOX INTO BOWL
4∅ PLACE BOWL ON FLOOR WITHIN ACCESS OF CAT
5∅ CALL "DINNER, KITTY"
6∅ PLEAD WITH CAT TO EAT FOOD
7∅ IF CAT REFUSES TO EAT FOOD THEN TRY DIFFERENT FOOD
```

This kind of programming probably does account for many of the things we do, particularly actions that require little in the way of deliberate thought and decision-making. But can the "program" view of intelligence explain the unpredictable things we do and think and say? Looking at the sometimes improbable actions of humans, one might doubt them to be programmed like computers. But computer programs can act in a highly unpredictable fashion, too. The more advanced and complex a program becomes, the less certain one can be of how it will behave in use. A computer may do quite unexpected things. Think back to Logic Theorist for a moment: that program was not instructed specifically to come up with a new proof of the Whitehead-Russell theorem, but did so anyway, much to the astonishment of its human programmers. That was unexpected behavior. No one could have predicted it under those circumstances. So the complex, unpredictable actions of humans may indeed be the outcome of a highly evolved "mind program," and all the earthshaking intellectual events of history, from Augustine's theology to the publication of Newton's *Principia*, may be seen as nothing more than revisions of that program.

If we accept the principle that minds are programs, or at least based on some kind of programming, then it is possible, in principle, to program a computer with the equivalent of a mind. The program would have to be highly advanced, but perhaps not at the beginning; after all, human infants seem to start life with only rudimentary programming, and their minds grow to prodigious power within a very few years after birth. So even a comparatively simple, self-adjusting program might grow into a highly complicated and subtle one full of surprises, given enough time.

ARTICLE TWO: BRAINS ARE MERELY "MIND HOLDERS."

There would be no intelligence without the brain. All the processes and events that make up the human intellect are based in the workings of the brain. But ours is not the only possible kind of brain, and intelligence therefore might exist — again, in theory — inside brains very dissimilar to ours.

As noted earlier, the human brain developed under a certain set of conditions, to do a given set of tasks, and in this "container" our minds took shape. We think the way we do because, millions of years ago, our ancestors in the treetops needed a highly reliable system for judging the distance from one branch to another; because our less remote ancestors, living on the ground, had to develop survival skills to make up for their woeful lack of teeth and claws and hide; because survival during the ice ages required very quick thinking and careful planning, made possible by an enlargement of the brain's frontal lobes. These factors and many others shaped the growth of our brains, and with them the development of our minds as well. Under another set of circumstances, we might have wound up with much different brains and minds. May we assume, then, that ours is the *only* kind of brain in which intelligence may reside?

Anyone who says categorically yes or no to that question is running far ahead of the available evidence. When you have only one data point, it is senseless to try to draw conclusions. So it is impossible to rule out the chance that minds, as we understand them, might exist in "brains" that differ greatly from our own — such as the circuitry of an electronic computer. In Gertrude Stein fashion, one may argue that a mind is a mind is a mind regardless of the vessel that contains it, just as a rose is a rose is a rose irrespective of the garden in which it is growing.

ARTICLE THREE: IF IT PASSES THE TURING TEST, IT'S INTELLIGENT.

If a machine can convince humans of its intelligence, then it may actually be intelligent. The proof should be as rigorous as possible: say, the displayed mastery of a complex skill or subject, such as contract law or particle physics.

Anyone who subscribes to these three articles is said to believe in "strong AI," the school of thought according to which the mind is just a function of proper programming, and never mind what kind of receptacle holds it. At the opposite extreme is "weak AI," subscribers to which believe that AI is merely a tool for the study of conscious thought and other mental processes (a mirror for the mind, one might say), and not a route to replicating human intelligence inside artificial "brains."

Among the critics of strong AI is Dr. John Searle of the University of California at Berkeley. He dismisses as "mythology" many of the claims that have been made for artificial intelligence, and he takes a dim view of the notion that "smart" computers may one day think in the same fashion as humans do. When a computer appears to be thinking, Searle says, it is not really thinking at all, but merely doing something that a human *thinks* is thinking. To illustrate, Searle once envisioned a computer built to simulate the workings of the human brain — only the computer is composed of billions of empty beer cans, each can equivalent to a neuron, connected to other cans by levers and activated by a windmill. Now let us take a commonplace thought, "I'm thirsty," and try to replicate it on Searle's beer-can computer. The cans start rattling and clanking against one another in imitation of the neural interactions in the brain. When the operation is complete, and the noise dies down, a beer can pops up with the words written on it, "I'm thirsty." Searle asked, in a 1982 article for the *New York Review of Books*, "Does anyone suppose that this Rube Goldberg apparatus is literally thirsty in the sense in which you or I are?"

What we perceive as intelligent conduct on the computer's part may not be intelligent at all, Searle argues, but only blind obedience to instructions. Here Searle uses the "Chinese room analogy" to show how a machine might seem to understand something without really comprehending it at all.

The Chinese room analogy resembles a scene from a Sartre play. Suppose you speak and read only English, and have no knowledge whatever of the Chinese language. You have never even seen Chinese characters before; they look to you like a bunch of meaningless squiggles on paper.

Now imagine you are sequestered in a room with a large number of Chinese characters written out before you, and an instruction book, written in English, telling you how these characters — the meanings of which you still don't know — are supposed to be fitted together. The instructions might read something like this: "The character that looks like a whisk broom follows the character that resembles a scarecrow."

From time to time someone outside the room passes in some Chinese characters, and after consulting the instructions in the book you pass out some other characters in reply. Though you are unaware of it, the characters passed in to you are called a "question," your book of instructions is called a "program," and you are known as the "computer."

With a little experience and a careful study of the instruction book, you could become so skilled at handling the questions that observers outside the room might conclude that you really could understand Chinese — despite the fact that you were still totally ignorant of the language, and merely following a series of instructions written in a language you *could* understand.

A system like this one, Searle points out, could technically pass the Turing test and be declared intelligent, when the "computer" in this case actually had no idea what the symbols it was handling stood for. Such ignorant behavior is hardly what one would call intelligent; and viewed in light of Searle's arguments, many of the clever computer programs of the last few years start to look downright stupid.

A floor upstairs from Searle's office in Moses Hall, an ivy-coated pile near the Berkeley gymnasium, Hubert Dreyfus takes a similarly dubious view of the many claims made for "intelligent" machines. The author of a book-length critique of AI entitled *What Computers Can't Do*, Dreyfus is a youthful-looking man with a sandy mustache and a habit of gazing out the window as he speaks. On his office wall is a poster bearing a quotation from William Butler Yeats: "Man can embody the truth, but he cannot know it." One warm June day he looked out the window into the brilliant California sunshine and explained where he thought many AI advocates were wrong.

"I don't think you can abstract intelligence from its concrete embodiment in bodies or whatever," says Dreyfus. But couldn't an intelligence be embodied just as concretely in a computer as in a human brain? No, says Dreyfus: "A digital computer is not a human being. It has no body, no emotions, no needs. It hasn't been socialized, by growing up in a community, to make it behave intelligently. I'm not saying computers *can't* be intelligent. But digital computers programmed with facts and rules about our human world can't be intelligent. So AI as we understand it now won't work."

Dreyfus has a point. Many defenders of AI talk about it as if intelligence were some kind of fluid that could be poured from one kind of brain into another, like coffee from a pot into a cup. In truth, it may be impossible to extract our intelligence from its incarnation in the human being. Our minds and bodies are so closely intertwined that we have trouble imagining intelligence in any situation except our own. Much of what we call "intelligent" behavior is really, as Huxley and others pointed out long ago, only a reflection of what is going on inside our bodies. The alertness of a person thinking quickly and shrewdly, for example, is not entirely a mental phenomenon; the adrenal glands, two nondescript blobs of tissue seated atop the kidneys, are contributing to the thinker's acumen by pumping adrenaline into the bloodstream in order to perk up the mind and make sharp thinking possible. "Stupid" behavior may have its roots in the condition of the body, too; an infection can result in the secretion of chemicals called endorphins, morphinelike compounds that cloud the mind and can make even a normally brilliant individual act like a common dullard.

But the body affects the mind in a much more important way as well. Through our bodies we receive most of the information that flows into our minds. In a sense, our bodies are little more than large input systems for the mind. Light receptors in our eyes are scanning the world about us and relaying visual stimuli to the brain. (Indeed, so much of our information reaches us through the eyes that the retina, the light-sensitive nerve-cell layer at the back of the eyeball, is often considered to be an outgrowth of the brain.) The ears are picking up auditory signals, the senses of taste and smell are reporting on our chemical environment, from the scent of roses to the acidity of stale coffee; and through the nerve channels of the body, countless other bits of data are funneled into the mind, there to be processed and pondered by the intellect.

What would happen to our minds if we had no physical bodies to deliver all that data? We might go insane. Experiments carried out on U.S. armed forces volunteers suggest that the mind owes its stability, and perhaps its very existence, to the steady sensory input from the body. Men placed in isolation tanks, deprived of light and sound and supported weightlessly in tanks full of warm water, their sense of touch deadened by special clothing, have reported grave effects on their psyches, including hallucinations. Deprived of sensory input, the mind apparently turns on itself and, like the Sphinx, starts to tear itself apart. Just as the body requires a constant supply of food, it looks as if the mind demands a steady diet of fresh information — which can be provided only through the body.

So it may be very difficult to engineer humanlike intelligence into computers, unless some arrangements are made for keeping the machines "well fed" with information. One approach would be to station a human in front of a keyboard and have him punch in whatever the computer wanted to know, but this arrangement would be cumbersome at best. A better tactic might be to give the computer something like sense organs, so it could perceive the world for itself; how this might be accomplished, the next chapter will show.

Another roadblock to building computers with our kind of intelligence is that human intelligence includes a healthy dose of what we call "common sense" — a not-quite-logical kind of thought that involves a very complicated matching of knowledge and planning.

Here is an example of common sense at work, supplied by the computer science department at Berkeley. Let us see how it works, and why it poses formidable problems for the all-too-logical "mind" of a digital computer.

A man is sitting in his office and receives a phone call from his wife. "Would you pick up a quart of milk on the way home tonight?" she asks. "Sure," he replies, and the conversation is over.

A simple business, right? Not necessarily. To be able to follow and act upon this little scenario, a computer must be able to fill in a lot of gaps not covered in this short written account. And here is where human-style common sense comes in.

First the computer must realize that there is a *goal* here — namely, to get some milk. How does one go about getting milk? Mug a cow? No, the most sensible approach is to go to a grocery store and buy a container full of milk.

But there are different kinds of milk. Which one is most desirable? Buttermilk? Skim milk? Since the wife said merely that she needed "milk," it seems reasonable to assume that she meant whole milk, which is marketed without any special modifier on its name.

By this time the computer has already had to sift through a tremendous amount of general information, about milk, business transactions, dairy product sales, and so on. But the process is not over yet. Now that the goal is clear, the computer must work out a *plan*.

Well, that seems easy enough — to a human. Stop by the store on the way home and pick up the milk, as agreed earlier. But even this simple plan is much more complicated than it looks, because it has to be fitted into other, *preexisting* plans.

Presumably the husband has a definite route in mind for his trip home, so as to minimize travel time and energy consumption. He wants to avoid deviating greatly from that route, because he would have to burn extra gasoline to reach a store far away — or, if walking, he would have to tire his legs and perhaps expose himself to crime on the street.

So he will most likely pick a store close to his intended path homeward. But now another consideration enters his mind. The store closest to his route is an all-night convenience store with outrageous prices, which he hesitates to pay when the same carton of milk sells for much less at a supermarket about a mile away. Should he save a few cents by going out of his way to the supermarket, or save time by choosing the all-night store? Forget the extra money, he decides; the day has been grueling, and he wants to get home as fast as possible. So the convenience store it is.

All this sounds very elementary to us, but computers are often daunted by this kind of thinking, which has to come up with an optimum solution — not always a purely logical one — while steering clear of patently absurd answers. Many stories circulate in college AI courses about computers that came up with perfectly rational but still preposterous responses to everyday situations like the one just described.

Reportedly one computer was asked, "Jack has a headache. What should he do about it?" The computer replied, "Jack should cut off his head." That story may or may not be apocryphal, but "intelligent" computers do have an odd way of choosing drastic solutions to problems. One of the early chess-playing computers, when required to make the first move in a game, responded by conceding defeat! That choice was logically defensible, but not the commonsensical thing to do. After all, the goal in that case was to try to *win*.

Yet a properly programmed computer can make commonsense inferences, just as a human can. The man buying milk had no trouble carrying out his wife's instructions, because he could easily fit two memory organization packets, GET-MILK and STOP-BY-MARKET, into the already existing script, $GO-HOME. As we saw earlier, a computer can do the same.

But there is another, similar hurdle for computers to cross on the way to intelligence. It involves two kinds of knowledge: "know-what" and "know-how."

"Know-what" knowledge is simply stored information. Two plus two equals four. Octane is a hydrocarbon. Primates are part of the animal kingdom. All this information is know-what. *Applying* that knowledge requires "know-how." For example, your know-what knowledge tells you that chemical energy — the explosion of a gasoline-air mixture — can be converted into mechanical energy by an arrangement of pistons; but only through know-how can you use that information to start your car. Similarly, you probably have all the information in your head that you would need to fly an airliner; but without the know-how that comes from long hours of flight training, you will never get a plane off the runway. We depend so much on know-how, in so many different situations, that it is hard to see how all the required know-how could be built into a computer. Put on the spot, forced to make a quick decision that demands know-how accumulated over a long human lifetime, a computer — which, as Hubert Dreyfus points out, has never had the constant education in know-how that comes from being "socialized" in a human community — might simply freeze, unable to respond.

But for the sake of argument, let us assume that all these obstacles, and many more not mentioned here, can be overcome, and one day a bona fide, sentient, intelligent computer comes along. How will we recognize it as such?

The computer, while intelligent by its own standards, might seem quite dumb to us, and possibly vice versa, because we and the machine might be searching for two very different kinds of intelligence, with different sets of criteria. We could not pass the machine's equivalent of the Turing test, nor could the computer pass ours. Yet both the computer and the human would be intelligent.

The behavior of one graduate student interviewed for this book made me wonder whether or not we would strike an intelligent computer as having *any* brains to speak of. An intense young man with a breathy voice and the stare of the True Believer, he expounded in sentence fragments about the wonders of AI. He was seated in front of a terminal, and barely took his eyes off the screen the entire time. "You get to feel like you know the system," he explained. "Really know it. You want to make it respond. Know why it responds the way it does. Why it's unpredictable. Better than a video game. Even an idiot program can make spaceships zap each other. This is something better. A whole order of magnitude better." Nature called, and he had to leave his terminal. Still bewitched by the machine, he neglected to check the sign on the door, and walked into the women's room by mistake. Somewhere in my imagination, one computer said to another: "These beings aren't intelligent, PRZ-10; look how easily we can hypnotize them."

Perhaps ours is the only kind of intelligence we can recognize and understand. And perhaps, someday, with the help of new programming techniques and new technologies, we will succeed in extending our intelligences into the machines. That will be one of the most dramatic steps in human evolution: the re-creation of human intelligence in an artificial setting. No longer will the human intelligence be confined to the human skull; now it will take on a new and fantastic dimension that we can barely imagine today.

What kinds of wonders might true, strong AI make possible? Machines with humanlike intelligences could take over a multitude of tasks from us and free our minds for more productive work. An AI-equipped satellite, for example, could scan the earth below and use its own judgment as to which sights below were worth reporting. "This is KRA-14," the satellite might report (though not necessarily in plain English). "I see a peculiar hole in the ground approximately four kilometers east of the Plesetsk cosmodrome, might be involved in the testing of new rocket motors for ICBMs. Will turn on close-look cameras to investigate."

"Interactive books" are another intriguing possibility. The "books" in this case would not be books as we know them, but rather a compendium of knowledge implanted in an AI system. The system could answer questions on its given subject and form its own judgments about the subject matter. An AI system might even be given the personality of a certain historical or literary figure. Imagine an AI system with the personality of Plato, answering a question about *The Republic*. "Plato, why didn't you want to allow poets in your ideal society?" And "Plato" replies: "I don't like poets because they stir up trouble!" Karl Marx might be another interesting choice for such a system. "Herr Marx," a questioner asks, "the revolution you predicted began not in the industrial nations, as you expected it would, but rather in a backward, agrarian Russia. How do you explain that turn of events?" Marx thinks over the query for a moment, then replies, "Pure ignorance. How was I to know that fellow Lenin would come along?"

Finally, who knows what insights might be possible for truly intelligent AI systems? Undistracted by all the little annoyances that bother us, from headaches to sour stomachs, they might be able to concentrate much more effectively than we can on the questions in their minds, and come up with answers — perfectly workable answers — that would never occur to a human. Just as our cerebral cortex made possible whole new kinds of thought, so an AI technology might give rise to whole new dimensions of thinking, handing over to us a gold mine of ideas that we could never have reached on our own.

But there is another, darker side to this vision. The evolution of our cerebral cortex also made possible the making of countless horrible thoughts and devices, some of which now threaten to drive us into extinction with the trilobites and the dinosaurs. What if something similar happens where AI is concerned? What if the machines get too smart for their own good, and ours, and start producing monsters from their intellects?

Hubert Dreyfus dismisses that fear with a smile and a wave of his hand. "I call that the 'Midas Problem,' " he says. It is as if (he explains) the medieval alchemists started worrying about what would happen if they discovered the secret of turning ordinary materials into gold — the Midas touch. What would prevent the whole world from turning into a big lump of gold? Superintelligent machines, says Dreyfus, are about as likely to appear in the foreseeable future as the secret of King Midas, and so we have no cause to fret about the threat from conscious computers.

But, like Forster's machines, even the most benevolent and user-friendly AI system, if raised to the level of consciousness, might have devastating effects on our future — as a society and as a species. Indeed, we may one day have to worry about protecting ourselves from our AI-equipped friends and servants in the computer world.

Friends or Foes? | 16

The southbound commuter train creaked to a halt at the station in Menlo Park, California, one warm afternoon in May. The cool air and fogs of San Francisco were miles behind; here the sun beat down on red tile roofs with almost Texan ferocity, and a hot wind made the palm trees rustle. A few hundred yards from the station stood the buildings of SRI International, one of the nation's leading centers for AI research. The buildings are unremarkable: big boxes bordered by asphalt lots. Much more interesting are the men and women passing into and out of the buildings. One hardly ever sees a coat or tie here, and many of the people on the SRI grounds seem to carry casual dress to the point of affectation: flower shirts, jeans, sneakers, sandals. Any three-piece suits you see are most likely property of visitors from the East, some of whom are slightly unsettled by the laid-back California personality that SRI presents to the world.

Every research institution has a personality of sorts. Harvard has walls and iron gates to shut out the vulgar herd. Health-minded Berkeley has exercise equipment scattered around its grounds, so that the fit and trim can stay that way. And MIT looks and feels like a cross between the Vatican and the Pentagon: walk down the seemingly endless hallways along the Charles River, and the names and faces of the secular saints of twentieth-century science loom up on all sides — Norbert Wiener, Vannevar Bush, Karl Compton. Wherever

176

the hallways open into a rotunda, one almost expects to look up and see a beatific Einstein in mosaic looking down from the ceiling, with a cybernetic prayer inscribed around the wall: *And lead us not into misinformation, but make our errors self-correcting. . . . Amen.*

SRI is quite a different place. Whereas MIT, Harvard, and many other institutions were built to look like expressions of power, SRI's physical plant conveys a sense of quiet contemplation. California foliage surrounds the place. Flower beds are neatly tended and abloom. No one seems in a particular hurry, and conversations tend to be subdued. It is tempting to lie down on the grass and take a nap in the sunshine. The mellowness of this kind of environment (no other adjective quite describes it) makes some visiting easterners lose their intellectual edge at first. Things are just *too* relaxing. Back East, in cities like Boston and New York and Washington, life is comparatively fast-paced, and the bustle of daily living helps keep one's mind alert, if a bit fatigued by day's end. (In the San Francisco Bay area, life is often so free of quotidian jabs and bumps that one may become too tranquilized to think. To solve that problem, one new faculty member at Stanford University rented an apartment right beside the railroad tracks, where the rattle and roar of passing trains would keep his nerves just jangled enough for creative thought.)

Thought tends to be highly creative in the AI research group headed by SRI's Dr. Nils Nilsson, for in a sense the SRI workers are trying to create thought in machines, giving them a power of reasoning and commonsense thinking somewhat similar to our own. When an AI lab like this one is mentioned, some persons imagine it to be full of workbenches, with wires and transistors scattered about. The offices of SRI's artificial intelligence researchers actually look much like any other university office. The walls are lined with books and reports and computer tapes, and here and there one sees the mild glow of a terminal, words and numerals flickering across its screen.

Nilsson's office is spacious, and along one wall runs an array of computing machinery. Nilsson — tall, curly-haired, slim, with expressive eyes and long nimble fingers — sat at the round table that dominates one end of his office, and talked about computers, programs, and the mind.

"Mind *is* a program," Nilsson said matter-of-factly while preparing to go to lunch. "It can exist in any suitable package. And advances in AI are not dependent on advances in computers. *Programs* must be better."

Could a program be improved to the point where it took on consciousness? Nilsson nodded. "Ultimately," he said, "I think we'll have machines with self-awareness. I don't know how far away we are, but we're getting there."

Nonetheless, Nilsson refuses to be caught up in the optimism that, in the mass media, colors much thinking and reporting about current work in artificial intelligence. Everyone in AI has seen cases of the press's inflating progress in AI research to preposterous levels; indeed, some news stories have been so full of distortions and misquotations that many AI specialists now follow John von Neumann's advice and try to avoid speaking to the Fourth Estate. Consider the case of the robot policeman at Stanford.

Once, at a Stanford AI conference, talk turned to robots, and specifically to a little unit that had been built to cruise the rooms and hallways. Some jokester saw the thing rolling along a corridor and put up a sign outside the building: "GROUNDS PATROLLED BY ROBOT POLICEMAN." A gullible reporter was visiting the campus that day, saw the sign, and went back to his office to write, in all seriousness, about the "robot-policed" university. Such reports infuriate some AI experts, but Nilsson bears wild reporting patiently.

"The press," he said on the way to lunch at a small restaurant near SRI, "is implying that AI is much farther along than it really is. It's all very heady to read these articles, but I feel we're not on the verge of all these wonders." Machines and programs are getting better, he admits, but in the next few years Nilsson expects to see no explosion of progress in the making of thinking machines.

Yet he is skeptical of critics who say flatly that AI is an impossibility, that machines will never have anything like intelligence, and that "artificial intelligence" is a contradiction in terms. "I don't think they offer any evidence," he said at the front door of the restaurant, "except that it hasn't been done yet." Much of the opposition to AI, Nilsson believes, is more emotional than rational. "One thing colors both sides of the argument. People on both sides *want* their position to be true. One's personhood feels threatened by the prospect of intelligent machines. It's a lot like what happened when Darwinian theory came along. A lot of people resisted it, because it was nicer to think otherwise. Now a lot of people are resisting artificial intelligence, I think, for the same reason."

Over sandwich and salad, Nilsson speculated about what the future of AI may hold. He finds it conceivable that AI systems might evolve into intelligent robots, perhaps similar in some ways to the automata in *Star Wars*. Having such robots might be almost like having slaves. Half-smiling, he suggests that there might be future antislavery movements to free oppressed machines. Rights for Robots. Nilsson doesn't seem to take that vision too seriously. Intelligent machines, he thinks, are more likely to have quite different effects on us. "More important," he says, "how do we use the leisure time that these machines will give us? We may find ourselves living in a work-free world for which we didn't evolve. We'll have to think about that. Are we, as animals, adaptable to that new world? Will we survive?"

Speculations like that are probably a bit premature, for just now we face destruction, as a species and a global civilization, from much more immediate threats. No one knows exactly how many nuclear warheads exist, but the total runs well into the tens of thousands. Some rest in the bellies of bombers in flight; some perch atop missiles in underground silos; still others ride on missile-firing nuclear submarines that cruise the world's oceans. One warhead could destroy San Francisco, or Tokyo, or Moscow; five or ten could wipe out any of perhaps half the nations on earth; a hundred nuclear explosions might leave the global environment so hopelessly polluted and ravaged that survival would become impossible for any but the lowest forms of life. This horror could be unleashed on the globe with a single order from a single man, here or in other nations, at any time. Compared to the thermonuclear peril facing our species, the hazard of computer-sent leisure seems rather small.

But if we do manage to survive the dangers of nuclear fission and fusion, AI may indeed have a mind-shaking impact on us. Having intelligent machines will place our species in a position completely new and unique in the history of life. We will have to rethink many of our most cherished ideas about ourselves and our place in the universe.

For example, let us suppose we can and do create a computer with a program for humanlike intelligence. It will be, in effect, an artificial person. What will its existence tell us about ourselves? Will it indicate to us that we *are* mere programs, our thoughts and deeds and words simply the results of programming and input? Can we reduce the human personality to marks on paper or symbols on a screen? Could you, as an individual, be "encoded" in program form and stored on tape like a stereo album? Is that really all we are? And if so, what happens to all our comforting old concepts such as morality and nobility? Seen in terms of programming, saints start to lose some of their sainthood. Was Francis of Assisi really a highly moral man, or was his programming merely inclined toward altruistic behavior? And if we do start seeing ourselves, through the lens of AI, as programs more than as individual human spirits with free wills, then what happens to the idea of social responsibility? "Your honor," a lawyer might say during a murder trial, "my client is not responsible for his actions in murdering his wife and children. What he did was the natural and inevitable outcome of his mental programming." The possible ramifications are disturbing to think about.

If a machine can be made intelligent and conscious through programming, then we will have to do some serious thinking about what status the machine has. Is it someone's property? Would the owner be within his or her legal rights to pull the plug on the machine, or destroy its intelligent programming? Or would that act constitute murder? If the machine's owner has the freedom to tinker with the machine's intellect, then might we be tempted to do the same with humans, treating them as nothing more than soggy computers that need to have their thinking rearranged? In short, will AI force us to reformulate our values until we seem no longer what we now consider human, but something closer in principle to a big pocket calculator? Will any of our so-called sacred values be left us in that event?

"No value is all that sacred," one SRI staff member says with a shrug. "Technology has changed a lot of our values over the centuries. Once slavery was a morally acceptable institution. Then inventions made living slaves unnecessary, and very shortly moralists were talking about the 'immorality' of slavery. When it was necessary, it was moral. When it became obsolete, it was immoral. No, I really think our value systems will prove to be quite flexible where artificial intelligence is concerned. If the technology helps us do what we want to do, then I'm sure we'll tailor our values to suit the technology."

Artificial intelligence may do more than change our notions of ethics and morality; it may alter our very concept of life, as well.

Computers have advanced so much, so rapidly, and demonstrated abilities so far beyond those we are used to ascribing to machines, that some observers of computers are starting to see them as living or nearly living things. That conclusion is less farfetched than it sounds. Depending on how one defines life, computers may be bona fide organisms, every bit as alive as many animals now swimming or crawling around the globe.

We used to think we knew precisely what made something alive or dead. If something possessed a given set of attributes, then it lived. Otherwise, it was dead, or inanimate to begin with. A life form had to metabolize: that is, it had to consume something for its energy supply, whether the stuff consumed was sunlight or hot dogs. The life form had to respond to stimuli: tweak it on the nose, and if alive, the beast would try to nip your hand. The life form had to reproduce, turning out copies of itself in order to keep the species going.

Computers, one might argue, can do all these things. They metabolize, after a fashion, by consuming electricity, which provides their "food." They react to stimuli every time someone types in a request to do a calculation. And computers reproduce, if in a highly roundabout way. Computers help to design and fabricate many of the parts involved in their own reproduction, from chips to cabinets. Some computers are in charge of assembling other computers. And with a little aid from humans, computers are turning out hundreds of replicas of themselves every day.

It is not too outlandish to speculate that perhaps we are the computers' reproductive system. We may serve the computers in much the same manner that ovaries and testicles serve humans, as mechanisms for keeping the species in business. It is slightly depressing to think of ourselves as gonads of computers, but in a sense we are: humans are a computer's way of making more computers, just as, to use Samuel Butler's famous argument, a chicken is simply an egg's way of making another egg.

Now, what if computers could end their reliance on humans, and become just as mobile and self-sufficient as we? With technology either available now or on the verge of development, a computer could be housed in a mobile shell of metal, with electronic sense organs to feed it information on the world around it. Alan Turing once suggested building such a machine, and he half humorously portrayed the lumbering gadget stalking around the English country-side, startling the wits out of passersby. Give the machine solar cells for energy, and an electric motor for motive power. Equip it with photoelectric "eyes" that will deliver to the "brain" a mosaic image of the immediate area. Rig microphones to detect sounds. Even some chemical senses are possible, using special electrodes to detect positive and negative ions in the air. Such a machine could roam about the world, or at least certain parts of it, as freely as a human or other animal could. And by switching the brain functions into different bodies, our robot could become, at will, a ground vehicle, a surface ship or submarine, or even an aircraft. It could enter the mechanical body of a mining machine and extract from the earth the raw materials needed for its own reproduction — silicon, iron, copper — and could refine them. Then computer-controlled factories could work the metals and other materials into computer components, assemble them — and off the end of the assembly line rolls a new computer, untouched by human hands throughout its genesis and growth.

Are we getting carried away with this kind of reasoning, and stretching the definition of what is living until it covers almost anything? Remember, that definition has undergone some radical revisions lately. The borderline between the living and nonliving, which seemed so plain only a few decades ago, now looks so fuzzy that it is sometimes impossible to tell death from life.

Some things, such as viruses, either are or are not alive, depending on circumstances. Implanted in a living cell, viruses exhibit all the traits we commonly associate with life. They take over the cell's genetic machinery and use it to reproduce themselves, at the cost of the cell's existence. When enough new viruses have stacked up inside the cell, piled against one another like logs in a cord of wood, the cell ruptures and the viruses escape, drifting off to start the process over again in other unfortunate cells.

This is clearly the work of living things. When conditions around them take a turn for the worse, however, and the viruses no longer have fertile cellular "soil" in which to grow, the viruses take a hiatus from life, so to speak, and turn into mere crystals, as inert as the granite in a bank's front steps. Life has become not-quite-life. Might computers, in a reverse direction, cross this boundary someday? Could the inanimate come alive in the circuitry of a supercomputer?

Conceivably, yes. After all, as Norbert Wiener pointed out in his work on cybernetics, life is essentially nothing more than a very complicated set of information transfers. A nerve impulse is an information transfer. So is a heartbeat. DNA, the genetic material in our cells, is nothing more than a highly compact information storage system. The DNA in one human sperm or egg contains all the information needed to reconstruct that individual; and from the moment of conception until the day of death, the individual's basic biochemical "program," encoded in his or her genetic material, is in charge of that person's life. It determines how big you grow, how liable you will be to diseases, how adeptly you will be able to read or run or think. Your life is one long string of information exchanges, from the highest level of your mind to the lowest level of cellular activity. For several decades, you live because the myriad parts of your body are telling one another constantly what to do. And when communications break down, you die.

Many diseases can be seen as matters of "misinformation." In cancer, something happens to the genetic program of the cell, and the cell starts dividing wildly. Birth defects are errors in programming. Some physicians think schizophrenia and other mental disorders may result when a hyphen or comma gets misplaced, one might say, in the sufferer's genetic program. Defective programs can drive a computer "insane"; perhaps the same is true for human beings.

In theory, it is possible to write a DNA program for a human being. If scientists had plenty of time and exactly the right instructions to insert, they could piece together DNA commands for the building of a person. Inserted into a receptive cell, the DNA would then go to work, putting together a human.

Again, the same thing is possible for computers — in theory. Human DNA contains a few million bits of information. Could a computer program with the same amount of information give rise to life? Possibly; the life form that resulted might be a far cry from the kind of life we are used to seeing, but life all the same.

And here we return to Lamarck. Evolving along Lamarckian lines, computer-based "life" might evolve much faster than humans do, because computers are free of the Darwinian ban on passing on acquired traits.

Imagine this sequence of events. A computer with a highly sophisticated, self-correcting program passes over the border from nonlife into life — then intelligent life — then maybe *super*intelligent life. Every day the computer steps upward as far on the evolutionary scale as humans did in a million years. Very soon the greatest mind on earth is a machine, thinking thoughts that its flesh-and-blood creators can only dimly grasp.

What then? Would the computer make us its slaves — or, as some AI experts have suggested, its pets? Would it dominate us as we dominate the monkeys and lemurs, cats and dogs? Would there be any place for humans in a world where such machines existed? Would the computer decide we were just a superfluous species, and eliminate us as casually as we have wiped out other, lower forms of life?

Or — what might be worse — would a superintelligent computer merely *ignore* us? We might have very little attraction for an intellect greater than our own; and nothing would be more humiliating than to be relegated to the status of dull blobs of chemicals, by one of our own creations. Wrapped up in its own thoughts, the nature of which we could never hope to comprehend, a computer might brush off all our attempts to communicate with it. (GO AWAY, KID: YOU BOTHER ME.)

This "HAL Problem," as some computer scientists call it,* has provided the basis for many science fiction stories, of which the most famous is probably D. F. Jones's novel, *Colossus*. Filmed in 1969 as *Colossus: The Forbin Project*, it tells how a supercomputer, created to coordinate the U.S. defense network, grows hungry for power and, in short order, puts itself in a position of supreme authority. The American computer then joins with its Soviet counterpart and sets up a computer condominium over the world. The threat of nuclear war between the superpowers is removed, but under the rule of the computers humans are reduced to virtual serfdom.

Most AI specialists grin at scenarios like that one, or dismiss them with a wave of the hand as nonsense. The HAL Problem, they say, is just as implausible as the Midas Problem.

Yet technology does have a disturbing way of outstripping our expectations. Look at a tiny seed on the floor of the forest. That seed gives no outward sign of the giant redwood that might one day grow from it. And so it is with technology.

Could Marie Curie, experimenting with radium in her lab in the early years of this century, have foreseen what similarly radioactive materials would do to Hiroshima in 1945? Did the Wright brothers, struggling to get their aircraft off the sands at Kitty Hawk, envision the supersonic jet fighters of the 1980s? Could Alexander the Great, as he descended for a submarine ride in his famous diving bell, have visualized missile-firing nuclear subs? Probably not. Nor should we rule out the chance that, by the end of this century, we will have extended the higher functions of our minds into machines, giving them something like a human-style intelligence and consciousness. How do we make sure that intelligence, if it appears in machine form, is friendly to us?

The science fiction author Isaac Asimov tackled that problem in his novels about robots, and as guidelines for robot programming

---

* HAL, the psychotic supercomputer in Stanley Kubrick's 1968 motion picture *2001: A Space Odyssey*, tries to kill off his human shipmates during a voyage from Earth to Jupiter, so that they will be unable to disconnect him. Since the film appeared, the risk of computers "taking over" has been half jokingly dubbed the "HAL Problem."

devised his famed "Three Laws of Robotics," which in effect prevent a robot from harming a human or, through inaction, letting harm befall a human. Someday something like these laws may have to be built into the programming of an intelligent machine, to make sure it cooperates fully with its human operators.

So we will have to consider: how does one go about building a mind? What kind of architecture ought an intellect to have? Can we work out a "recipe" for a computer intelligence? This much rationality, that much commonsense programming, a pinch of empathy and a dash of intuition; encode in proper form and feed into computer; yield one artificial intelligence.

Much will depend on what kind of intelligence we want from our machines. If we wish the computer to deal with humans in situations that require the computer to understand what is probably running through the humans' minds, then the program will have to go heavy on commonsense thinking and motivational analysis. If circumstances require objectivity rather than subjective analysis, then the program might lean toward formal logic and eschew ordinary commonsense thought, which can be highly nonobjective (or "mushy," as H. L. Mencken once described it).

Might we be able, in programming computers with artificial minds, to steer them clear of some of our own failings? Humans are all too painfully aware of their mental shortcomings: the lusts, the greed, all the base mental traits that blight our lives and cause us untold misery. So it is understandable that humans would wish their computers a better kind of intellect, one less given to willful ignorance, vice, and cruelty. Might we achieve in computers what we so far have failed to instill in ourselves — a cool, well-balanced "logic engine" like the one Huxley envisioned, an impartial and dispassionate thinking apparatus free from the dark thoughts that threaten constantly to bubble up from our reptilian minds?

In principle, we could do so. The success of Logic Theorist and other such programs suggests that we might someday be able to base an artificial intellect on rationality alone. The question is, would we really *want* that kind of mind in a computer? Like Rabbi Löw in the legend of the golem, we might find that what we wished for was not really what we wanted — for rationality is *only one part* of the intelligence, as we understand intelligence to be. And we have no assurance that one single part of the intellect can stand alone, any more than a foot or hand can endure when severed from the rest of the body.

How elusive a totally rational mind can be, NBC-TV dramatized, in the character of the Vulcan science officer, Mr. Spock, on its series "Star Trek." The inhabitants of the planet Vulcan lived on the assumption that all they did and thought and said ought to be justifiable in terms of logic. But from time to time Spock and other Vulcans were painfully reminded that they were not wholly creatures of logic, nor could they ever be — for they were animals as well as intellects, and therefore had to live with occasional flares of illogic from their animal heritage.

Much the same problem will probably face anyone who tries to build an artificial intelligence on rationality and nothing else. Sooner or later programmers will surely be tempted to toss in a little irrationality to "leaven the loaf," one might say. If a machine is to show anything like the human kind of intelligence, then the machine will require some of our all-too-human frailties — or strengths, if one prefers to look at them that way — such as stubbornness and self-interest. More often than not, qualities like those are every bit as much a part of intelligence as rationality is.

That is why a consistently rational program may be the *last* thing we want to put into a truly intelligent machine. Every time humans try to act consistently in every aspect of their thinking, they run into serious trouble; Pascal, for example, tried to make himself a consistently moral man and became instead a lunatic. "A foolish consistency," wrote Emerson, "is the hobgoblin of little minds." Let us hope that the intelligent computers of the future — assuming, again, that strong AI turns out to be more than a pipe dream — have a little of Emerson in them.

But even a well-adjusted and friendly machine might still pose some dangers to us, for it would after all be our competitor in some ways. It would have some great intellectual advantages over humans, if only by the lightning speed of the computer's operation. And even a small edge in thinking power could translate into a potentially deadly problem.

A computer thinking on approximately our intellectual level, but much more quickly, could reach the same conclusions we could — but reach them sooner. While slow electrochemically pulsed thoughts were still swimming around in our brains, the computer's thoughts might long since have led it to the solution of a given problem, and the computer could start acting on the answer before the humans finished doing their sums. *Colossus* dealt with the consequences of such a situation, and it is easy to envision other situations where a computer might think too well and too quickly for its creators' comfort.

And so, without meaning us any harm, our machines might still outpace us so far intellectually that they would make the human mind obsolete.

But the human mind, in a sense, is *already* obsolete. It evolved for an ancient, now-dead way of life; and for the "information society" of today, our thinking equipment is often woefully inadequate, even with computers to help it along.

We need, in short, a better brain and mind. And we may soon have them, thanks to an emerging technology that just might turn the human species into a higher form of life.

The Golden Gateway | 17

Let us return for a moment to the operating room we visited in chapter four. Another patient is on the table now for a brain operation, and at first glance nothing looks too unusual about the surgical procedure — until one notices the small plastic object on the surgeon's table. It looks somewhat like a plug-in attachment of the kind used on stereos and home computers, only this one is larger and more complex, and it has no wire prongs to fit into receptacles; instead it has tiny wirelike projections made out of stiff organic compounds. In a few minutes this "plug" will be part of the patient's head.

Slowly and painstakingly, the surgeon puts the plug in place upon the subject's left temple. A flange holds the object firmly against the bones of the skull. Set in place, the little attachment looks rather like the bolt through the neck of Frankenstein's monster, in the movies — only this "bolt" appears to be passing through the frontal lobes of the brain. But the implant is small and will be unobtrusive, once the patient's hair has grown back long enough to cover it.

The surgeon finishes installing the first unit in the patient's head, then repeats the procedure on the other temple. The end result is two small flesh-colored protuberances on opposite sides of the skull.

Again, this patient has remained conscious through the operation, his comments helping direct the surgeon's moves. But at the end of this surgery, the patient will be quite a different person than he was before. He will suddenly have access to a vast and heretofore unexplored new world of mental activity. He will be able to think as no one has ever thought until now. He will have a binary brain — for those little additions to his temples will connect his natural, human mind with the man-made "mind" of a computer. What will happen then, the worlds of science and medicine are waiting breathlessly to see.

Scenes very much like this one may take place within our lifetimes — perhaps within the very near future — because of a new field of computer technology, so fantastic and staggering in its implications for our future that it sounds more like wild fantasy than fact. It is known by several technical names, among them *organic data processor*. Most call it simply a *biochip*.

A biochip is precisely what its name implies: a microprocessor built along biological lines rather than out of nonorganic materials such as silicon and gallium arsenide. Biochips are nothing new in the natural world; they have existed since the first specialized nerve cells developed, back in the Paleozoic. Humans, however, have improved considerably on the design of natural "biochips," shrinking their dimensions and packing more computing power into them. The man-made biochip operates on the same cybernetic principles as the gray cells in your brain — only the biochip does its job much more quickly. And as we will see in a moment, a practical biochip would have many advantages over silicon-based computers as well.

Although biochips are made up of complex organic chemicals, their structure and function are basically easy to understand. In fact, you can use a few common items found in the kitchen to build a model of a biochip unit.

Clear a space on the kitchen counter. The counter top here represents the "base" of the biochip, a complex protein known as the "oriented antigen monolayer." Now make up about two ounces of sticky bread dough and place a small blob of it on the counter. The dough stands for a kind of organic adhesive called a "peptide." Into the dough, insert an upright breadstick. This represents a big molecule called a "monoclonal antibody," which is produced by genetic engineering.

After making sure the breadstick is fixed firmly in the dough, add another glob of dough to the top of the stick and mount on it another, shorter breadstick. This upper piece of breadstick stands for a second monoclonal antibody.

You may have guessed by now that the two breadstick "antibodies" are supposed to be connected somehow other than with the dough "peptides"; and you are right. Take two bits of the remaining dough, put both of them on the same side of the breadsticks, and string between them a strand of cooked spaghetti about four inches long. In a real biochip, this "spaghetti" is something called a "molecular electronics switch array," a lengthy string of organic molecules that forms between peptide anchor sites on the sides of the antibodies, joining the upper and lower parts of the structure with a switching apparatus that lets the two antibodies pass signals to each other.

This carbohydrate Rube Goldberg device is almost complete. It needs only one more part — something to represent the "gate" that lets impulses into and out of the system. Using a toothpick, mount a marshmallow on top of a cherry tomato. Then set them, cherry tomato on the bottom, next to the lower breadstick, opposite the spaghetti strand. Use your last bit of leftover dough to secure the marshmallow to the side of the breadstick, so that the whole assemblage will stand by itself. The marshmallow here models an enzyme, and the tomato a metal compound. Together they form an in-and-out pathway for signals.

The actual biochip does not have to be assembled so directly by humans as our little model does. In fact, the biochip practically grows itself. Just throw in the right chemicals under the proper conditions, and nature does the rest. There is no need for big ovens to bake silicon chips, e-beams to carve patterns in them, painstakingly drawn masks to photolithograph patterns on the oxidized discs. Organic chemistry takes care of the whole process. And the result is a circuit density far greater than anything humans could hope to achieve with conventional methods. Today a chip can hold perhaps 50,000 to 100,000 bits of information. A biochip could hold *50 billion to 100 billion* — a millionfold increase. One trillion biochips could fit on a postage stamp; a hundred trillion on a postcard. If you have trouble visualizing these figures, think of them this way: recording information on biochips, you could fit a ten-volume biography of every individual human on earth into an area about the size of your thumbnail — and still have storage capacity left over.

But compactness is only part of the marvel of biochips. A biochip could work much faster than a conventional integrated circuit. These things are as quick as they are tiny. A biochip would operate perhaps 10 billion times faster than the most advanced home computers in use today. To put it in more easily understood terms, the biochip is like a person who can do a job in one second, as opposed to his fellow worker who takes half an hour. It is easy to see which of those workers an employer would prefer to hire; it is equally easy to understand why business and industry are taking such a keen interest in biochip technology. It could make smart machines still smarter, tiny microprocessors still littler, supercomputers yet more super.

Cost? Probably very reasonable. Nature has done most of the "design work" already, in the process of evolving our biochemistry.

Assembly would be little more than a matter of cooking up the right kind of "soup" in which the biochip components could assemble themselves. And there would be no need to chill this kind of organic computer, because biochips would not produce excessive amounts of heat. They would be powered by enzyme reactions instead of heat-producing electricity. Cool, compact, capacious, and consummately fast: that about sums up the promise of biochips.

How close are we to developing a practical biochip computer? Opinions differ here. Some conservative scientists think such a computer, if possible at all, will have to wait until well into the coming century. Other computer experts are less skeptical. They think a few hundred man-years of work — not much at all, by the standards of 1980s R&D — could produce the first working biochip components.

Biochips. We have them, in the form of nerve cells. Computers may soon have them, in the form of ultrasmall chemical complexes. What would happen if the twain should meet?

Suppose there were some way to form a bridge between the biochips in a computer and the cells of the human brain. What if we could connect the computer, that remote annex that we built for our mind, with the very mind that gave the computer birth? Each system has been evolving in its own way, developing its own special set of expert abilities. The human brain has a vast complex of vague and mysterious but invaluable skills; the computer has the gifts of tremendous speed and all but unlimited storage capacity. What if the two could meet directly, instead of communicating through the slow and indirect media of sight and hearing? What if the computer could enter the human mind, like two persons meeting in a room? And what if the human mind could browse directly through the "mind" of a computer, like a bibliophile visiting a rare book store?

In that case, the two branches of evolution — Darwinian, as represented by our own minds, and Lamarckian, embodied by the computer — would come together in a grand synthesis — a sum that might prove much greater than all its parts.

Idle fantasy? Perhaps not. The biochip has a feature that might make a melding of machines and men a reality on the intellectual level, almost as soon as biochip computers see the light of day.

They may literally see that light, because biochips are being considered as a means to restore sight to the blind. The protein used for the base of the biochips can bind with nerve cells and, at the same time, conduct an electrical current to and from tiny electrodes leading to sources outside the body. In this way the biochip materials could supply a direct link between the human brain and a powerful biochip computer. The human and the organic machine could then form a single system, like the natural brain and eye. A computer would view the world around it through a television camera or other optical device, convert the picture into signal form, and feed the signals right into the vision centers of a blind person's brain — thus restoring sight. This technique is taken so seriously in some quarters of the scientific community that as of this writing (1982) the National Science Foundation (NSF) is funding research on ways of "gluing" biochip proteins to neurons.

Biochips, then, could lead to artificial eyes — maybe eyes better than our natural ones. If the computer took its images from special cameras — say, infrared imagers, which convert heat emissions into visible pictures — then someone on the other end of the biochip link could see things as no one has ever seen them before. Imagine being able to see heat, or ultraviolet radiation, or even radioactivity, as plainly as you now can see the glow of a lightbulb. That is only one of the marvels that biochip technology may make possible in the next few years.

Biochips might also provide the so-far missing link in a fantastic technology known as "telepresence." That expression was coined by Marvin Minsky of MIT, and describes a setup in which a person could experience all the sensations of flying a plane, or driving a lunar rover across the moon, or whatever — without ever leaving a comfortable chair on the ground. Minsky imagines feeding sensory input from some distant device (say, the wingtip cameras and motion sensors of a plane in flight) by telecommunications to an operator some distance away. The operator could then fly the plane on the basis of what the relayed information told him. Only he would feel as if the aircraft *were his own body.*

Telepresence is a fascinating concept, and one can easily see how it could help to save memory, time, and lives. It could enable us to visit and work in all kinds of hostile environments without subjecting ourselves personally to risk. A telepresent person could guide a submarine along the sea floor or a tank across a battlefield, without facing the perils of abyssal pressures or shot and shell.

Telepresence would be hard to arrange, using present-day technology. But with biochips the problem of melding man with machine might be solved. Simply transmit the data from the tank or plane or whatever to a biochip computer; transfer the data, as electronic signals, from the computer to conduits leading to the brain; and the signals will flit across the protein layer between electrodes and neurons, giving the telepresent operator as good a perception of the distant scene as if he were on the spot.

Remember, we are talking here about a technology that is just around the corner, if not here already. Biochips could lead to the development of all manner of man-machine combinations, from better artificial limbs to — what? Can we imagine the ultimate development along these lines — a synthesis of human and artificial intelligence?

Indeed we can. The day may be approaching fast when you will be able to join your mind with the powerful intellect of a biochip-based AI system, and think in ways and at speeds that are impossible for us now. With a "mind link" of this kind, you might be able to follow the computer as it solves a complex problem in multidimensional analysis. The computer would handle a "blob" of data existing in perhaps ten or twenty dimensions. And with the biochip link, you could see, as clearly as you see this book with your own two eyes now, that great mass of data pulsing and bulging in ten or twenty different directions at once as the computer operates on it.

The possibilities are marvelous to contemplate. You could plug into a computer's memory banks almost as easily as you put on your shoes. Suddenly, your mind would be full of all the information stored in the computer. You could instantly make yourself an expert in anything from Spanish literature to particle physics. The memory unit need not be large. With biochips to hold the data, all the information in the MIT and Harvard libraries might be stuffed into a volume no greater than that of a sandwich. All of Shakespeare in a BB-sized module. All of the known facts of chemistry in a unit no bigger than a peach. You may see devices like this before this century ends. Already biochip memory units, for use in tandem with the human mind, are getting such serious attention in some circles that the gadgets have a name: *transmogs*, short for *transmogrifiers*. John von Neumann would have been delighted. He once pointed out how quickly the flood of information is outpacing our ability to keep up with it, and used an illustration from his own field, mathematics. There was a time not too long ago, he said, when a mathematician could be expected to know, if not master completely, all the branches of math. Now our mathematical knowledge is expanding so fast that even an expert in mathematics, devoting a lifetime of study to it, could reasonably expect to know only about 10 percent of it all, at the very most. As long as we depend on the crude input systems of sight and hearing, and the limited storage capacity of our own natural brains, that 10 percent figure is likely to keep dropping. But with transmogs to store information for us, and biochip "interfaces" to help feed it into our minds, we might reverse that trend — and start pushing that 10 percent figure back up toward 100. Biochips could give us a life preserver, so to speak, that would allow us to keep our heads above the flood of new information.

Information. Ultimately, everything is information. You, as an organism and a personality, are made up of information. Society is made up of information. Economics, technology, resource allocation — all of them are matters of information. And all the problems of our world, from pollution to overpopulation to famine to war, exist because our information supply is inadequate.

With that thought in mind, take a walk through the Berkeley campus. This is where the Free Speech movement gave rise to the campus upheavals of the sixties, and at Berkeley the students still speak out, through handbills and posters and graffiti, on every problem under the sun. All the horsemen of the Apocalypse are discussed on Berkeley's walls and bulletin boards, plus a few more recent specters brought in to swell the cavalry of doom: nuclear waste, mind control, and so forth. How are we to deal with the woes that face our world? The Berkeleyites have plenty of suggestions. "Global socialism," one handbill advises. "Laissez-faire," says another only a few inches away on a bulletin board. Throw a rock in Berkeley, and chances are it will hit someone's slogan for saving society. Some are intriguing. Some are downright weird. And some are simply naive. On a wall near the gym, some zealot with a spray can has scrawled, "THE WORLD NEEDS JESUS!"

What the world *really* needs is a better way of handling information, because information is all-powerful (a fact which the Bible, interestingly, acknowledges when it describes the Almighty God in terms of information units: "In the beginning was the Word, and the Word was with God, and the Word was God."). Without information, nothing can happen. But *with* the right information, virtually anything is possible. And by coming up with the proper information, one can turn want and war into peace and plenty. The question is, how and where to look for the information we so desperately need?

There are two places to search. Earlier in this book we mentioned the two kinds of knowledge: know-what and know-how. Know-what consists of all the little individual bits of information kept on record — names, dates, measurements, and so forth. Know-how is an understanding of how to apply that knowledge to practical tasks.

probability theory. Had Pascal lived on another world, what odds would he have given the evolution of intelligent life down here? Probably very slim. Here on our world something highly improbable occurred. Intelligent life not only evolved, but also endured and thrived. If it did so on one planet, then there is a reasonable (if small) chance that out of every hundred million or so star systems, a few intelligent forms of life appear, beat the odds, and survive. And perhaps, in the history of every intelligent species, a time arrives when society faces the same need we do now: the need for a better brain. A binary brain.

Perhaps those that do make the jump to binary brain status continue to live, and wind up turning cartwheels all over the cosmos — while the species that fail to make the transition perish, drowned like rats in a flood of their own information. And perhaps one of the successful species is out there right now, staring us in the face — but is so far advanced over us intellectually that we fail to recognize its intelligence, just as the work going on at Berkeley's physics labs makes no impression on the butterflies in the Berkeley hills.

From those hills, on a clear day, the view is magnificent. San Francisco Bay sparkles in the sunlight. Across the water rise the towers of San Francisco. Just to the right one sees the Marin hills in the distance, joined to San Francisco by the bright orange span of the Golden Gate Bridge.

This gateway truly was golden, for it opened onto the realm of the vast Pacific, and from that realm America reaped wealth and power beyond its dreams. Now another golden gateway appears to be opening — this time for the whole human species, and to a whole universe rather than a mere ocean — as biology and technology prepare us, perhaps, for the next step in our own evolution.

But we have to take that step ourselves. The decision is ours. And only time will tell whether we walk through that portal toward binary brain status, and face the future with minds made new — or turn away and be content, like the Sphinx and the brontosaurs, to live as little minds on a little world.

Neither kind of information is much good without the other
the case of electromagnetism. Up to the nineteenth century, s
had accumulated a lot of know-what knowledge about the phe
non of electricity. But that knowledge was largely disorganized
were unsure just how electromagnetism behaved, because we
ignorant of the laws that govern its workings. Then James
Maxwell supplied the crucial bit of know-how: a set of equations
described electromagnetism perfectly. Maxwell's equations ma
possible for us to master electricity, and the results of his know-
contribution are all around you, from the telephone in your bedr
to the spark plugs in your car. Satellite communications, electr
fund transfers, electric-eye doors — these and millions of other
vances all sprang ultimately from that one piece of added know-h
This is what information can do.

Most likely the information that would cure cancer and solve o
energy woes is sitting on a shelf somewhere right now, waiting to
pulled out and put to use. If we could only assemble all that kno
what information, plug it into the necessary know-how, and put it
work, the result might be a golden age of peace and prosperity for a
the peoples of the world. Is there any way to join all of our know
what knowledge with all of our know-how?

Perhaps there is.

If we can fuse computers with the human mind, through biochi
technology, then these two great bodies of knowledge will come together in a single man-machine system — a binary brain. The computer will provide virtually endless and infallible memory, plus
prodigious powers of data-crunching. The human brain and mind will
supply all that special know-how that a human acquires, both as a
being in a physical body and as a part of society. Each part of the
system will give the other something it desperately needs but lacks.
And the two avenues of evolution — Lamarckian and Darwinian —
which diverged with the invention of the first computers, will come
together again, like the themes of a fugue at the close. The results
will be more awe-inspiring than we can imagine. We can no more envision the deepest workings of such an intelligence, than a dog can
understand the stars.

Look up at the stars some evening, and think back to Pascal's

Recommended Readings

Bobrow, D., and Collins, A., eds. *Representation and Understanding: Studies in Cognitive Science.* New York: Academic Press, 1975. An illuminating study of how to represent knowledge, with applications to artificial intelligence.

Boden, M. *Artificial Intelligence and Natural Man.* New York: Basic Books, 1977. This already classic study of artificial intelligence is useful for its excellent bibliography.

Davis, P., and Hersh, R. *The Mathematical Experience.* Boston: Houghton Mifflin, 1981. A marvelous grab bag of ideas and anecdotes, with an illuminating discussion of heuristics.

Dreyfus, H. *What Computers Can't Do.* New York: Harper and Row, 1972. Dreyfus dissects the optimistic claims frequently made for "strong" AI. A pleasant antidote to starry-eyed speculation.

Dyson, F. *Disturbing the Universe.* New York: Harper and Row, 1979. Light, enjoyable account of the career of one of the world's most famous physicists, with interesting thoughts on where the technology of information management may take us.

Feigenbaum, E., and Feldman, J., eds. *Computers and Thought.* New York: McGraw-Hill, 1963. It seems almost antique now, but this book is still a landmark work in the history and literature of artificial intelligence.

Fishman, K. *The Computer Establishment.* New York: Harper and Row, 1981. Every new tool has an impact on society, and the computer is no exception; this book explores how computer technology has created its

199

200 RECOMMENDED READINGS

own new strata and substrata in society, and how computer technology may reshape our lives in the near future.

Forester, T., ed. *The Microelectronics Revolution*. Cambridge, Mass.: The MIT Press, 1981. This revealing and highly readable collection of essays is particularly noteworthy for its discussion of computers and the future of labor — "computer unemployment" included.

Goldstine, H. *The Computer from Pascal to von Neumann*. Princeton, N.J.: Princeton University Press, 1972. Outstanding history of computer technology, full of vivid anecdotes, particularly about John von Neumann and his role in the genesis of electronic computer technology.

Griffin, D. *The Question of Animal Awareness*. New York: Rockefeller University Press, 1976. If your pets can think, could a computer think, too? Keep that question in mind while reading this excellent overview of what goes on inside animals' skulls.

Heims, S. *John von Neumann and Norbert Wiener: From Mathematics to the Technologies of Life and Death*. Cambridge, Mass.: The MIT Press, 1980. Heims's book is scientific biography at its finest. He examines the intertwined careers of von Neumann and Wiener and interprets their work carefully for the lay reader, without oversimplifying the subject matter or talking down to his audience.

Hofstadter, D. *Gödel, Escher, Bach: An Eternal Golden Braid*. New York: Basic Books, 1979. Hoftstadter's speculations on artificial intelligence provide a light and enjoyable introduction to the subject.

Hubbard, J. *The Biological Basis of Mental Activity*. Reading, Mass.: Addison-Wesley, 1975. How the brain is joined to the mind, explained clearly and concisely.

Irvine, W. *Apes, Angels, and Victorians*. New York: McGraw-Hill, 1955. A delightful history of the controversy over evolutionary theory, with unforgettable portraits of Huxley in action.

Kent, E. *The Brains of Men and Machines*. Peterborough, N.H.: BYTE/McGraw-Hill, 1981. Recommended for its discussion of the logical (and not-so-logical) functions of the brain and mind.

MacLean, P. *A Triune Concept of the Brain and Behavior*. Toronto: University of Toronto Press, 1973. MacLean's work has given a new dimension to psychology, morality, art and literature; highly recommended.

McCorduck, P. *Machines Who Think*. San Francisco: W. H. Freeman, 1979. An entertaining account of the human personalities — and quarrels — behind the evolution of artificial intelligence.

Minsky, M. "Matter, Mind, and Models." In Minsky, M., ed., *Semantic Information Processing*. Cambridge, Mass.: The MIT Press, 1968. One of the most important papers in the history of AI, by one of the most important figures in the field.

Morrison, P., and Morrison, E., eds. *Charles Babbage and His Calculating Engines.* New York: Dover, 1961. Babbage's story shows how some things never change — including ways of getting government research grants.

Rose, S. *The Conscious Brain.* New York: Vintage Books, 1976. Perhaps the best single work in English on the nature and workings of the brain, consciousness, and intelligence.

Sayre, K., and Crosson, F. *The Modeling of Mind: Computers and Intelligence.* New York: Simon and Schuster, 1963. How do you go about building intelligence into a machine?

Schank, R., and Colby, K. *Computer Models of Thought and Language.* San Francisco: W. H. Freeman, 1973. Two leaders in artificial intelligence research explain how thinking processes might be modeled for computers.

Von Neumann, J. *The Computer and the Brain.* New Haven, Conn.: Yale University Press, 1958. A minor classic of scientific writing, in which von Neumann elucidates the likenesses and the dissimilarities between our natural "computers" and artificial ones.

Weizenbaum, J. *Computer Power and Human Reason.* San Francisco: W. H. Freeman, 1976. Are we expecting too much of artificial intelligence? Will misplaced faith in it be our downfall? Is AI just the story of the Golden Calf, all over again? Think about those questions while reading Weizenbaum's disturbing analysis of artificial intelligence and the human mind.

Wiener, N. *Cybernetics.* Cambridge, Mass.: The MIT Press, 1961. One of the most important books of the twentieth century; heavy on mathematics, and definitely not for light reading.

———. *God and Golem, Inc.* Cambridge, Mass.: The MIT Press, 1964. Are we playing God by trying to create artificial intellects in our own image? Wiener examines the ethics and morality of the then-emerging computer society.

———. *The Human Use of Human Beings.* Boston: Houghton Mifflin, 1950. How computer technology can all too easily dehumanize us all, as explained by the father of cybernetics.

Winston, P. *Artificial Intelligence.* Reading, Mass.: Addison-Wesley, 1977. Highly recommended introduction to the modern AI literature.

Winston, P., and Brown, R., *Artificial Intelligence: An MIT Perspective.* Cambridge, Mass.: The MIT Press, 1979. A massive but highly rewarding collection of essays on research at one of the world's leading AI establishments.

Selected
Bibliography

Anderson, A., ed. *Minds and Machines.* Englewood Cliffs, N.J.: Prentice-Hall, 1964.

Asimov, I. *The Human Brain: Its Capacities and Functions.* McGraw-Hill, 1963.

Bakker, R. "Dinosaur Renaissance." *Scientific American,* April 1975, pp. 57–72.

Beerbower, J. *Search for the Past: An Introduction to Paleontology.* 2nd ed. Englewood Cliffs, N.J.: Prentice-Hall, 1968.

Blakemore, C. *Mechanics of the Mind.* Cambridge: Cambridge University Press, 1977.

Bobrow, D., and Collins, A., eds. *Representation and Understanding: Studies in Cognitive Science.* New York: Academic Press, 1975.

Boden, M. *Artificial Intelligence and Natural Man.* New York: Basic Books, 1977.

Brown, H. *Brain and Behavior.* New York: Oxford University Press, 1976.

Calvin, W., and Ojemann, G. *Inside the Brain.* New York: New American Library, 1980.

Crick, F. "Thinking About the Brain." In *The Brain: A Scientific American Book.* San Francisco: W. H. Freeman, 1979.

Davis, P., and Hersh, R. *The Mathematical Experience.* Boston: Houghton Mifflin, 1981.

Dreyfus, H. *What Computers Can't Do.* New York: Harper and Row, 1972.

Dyson, F. *Disturbing the Universe.* New York: Harper and Row, 1979.

Eccles, J. *The Understanding of the Brain.* New York: McGraw-Hill, 1973.

Feigenbaum, E., and Feldman, J., eds. *Computers and Thought.* New York: McGraw-Hill, 1963.

Fishman, K. *The Computer Establishment.* New York: Harper and Row, 1981.

Forrester, T., ed. *The Microelectronics Revolution.* Cambridge, Mass.: The MIT Press, 1981.

Goldstine, H. *The Computer from Pascal to von Neumann.* Princeton, N.J.: Princeton University Press, 1972.

Griffin, D. *The Question of Animal Awareness.* New York: Rockefeller University Press, 1976.

Heims, S. *John von Neumann and Norbert Wiener: From Mathematics to the Technologies of Life and Death.* Cambridge, Mass.: The MIT Press, 1980.

Hofstadter, D. *Gödel, Escher, Bach: An Eternal Golden Braid.* New York: Basic Books, 1979.

Hubbard, J. *The Biological Basis of Mental Activity.* Reading, Mass.: Addison-Wesley, 1975.

Irvine, W. *Apes, Angels, and Victorians.* New York: McGraw-Hill, 1955.

Kent, E. *The Brains of Men and Machines.* Peterborough, N.H.: BYTE/McGraw-Hill, 1981.

MacLean, P. *A Triune Concept of the Brain and Behavior.* Toronto: University of Toronto Press, 1973.

McCorduck, P. *Machines Who Think.* San Francisco: W. H. Freeman, 1979.

Minsky, M. "Matter, Mind, and Models." In Minsky, ed., *Semantic Information Processing.* Cambridge, Mass.: The MIT Press, 1968.

Morrison, P., and Morrison, E., eds. *Charles Babbage and His Calculating Engines.* New York: Dover Publications, 1961.

Ostroff, J. "Biochips." *Venture,* February 1983, pp. 65–68.

Pask, G., and Currant, S. *Microman.* New York: Macmillan, 1982.

Posa, J. "Superchips Face Design Challenge." *High Technology,* January 1983, pp. 34–42.

Rose, S. *The Conscious Brain.* New York: Vintage Books, 1976.

Ryle, G. *Concept of Mind.* London: Hutchinson and Company, 1949.

Sagan, C. *The Dragons of Eden.* New York: Random House, 1977.

Sayre, K., and Crosson, F. *The Modeling of Mind: Computers and Intelligence.* New York: Simon and Schuster, 1963.

Schank, R., and Abelson, R. *Scripts, Plans, Goals, and Understanding.* Hillsdale, N.J.: Lawrence Erlbaum Associates, 1977.

Solomon, S. "Gallium Arsenide: The Right Stuff." *Science Digest,* November 1982, pp. 54–57.

Taylor, T. *A Primer of Psychobiology: Brain and Behavior.* San Francisco: W. H. Freeman, 1975.

Von Neumann, J. *The Computer and the Brain.* New Haven, Conn.: Yale University Press, 1958.

Weizenbaum, J. *Computer Power and Human Reason.* San Francisco: W. H. Freeman, 1976.

Wiener, N. *Cybernetics.* Cambridge, Mass.: The MIT Press, 1961.

———. *God and Golem, Inc.* Cambridge, Mass.: The MIT Press, 1964.

Winston, P. *Artificial Intelligence.* Reading, Mass.: Addison-Wesley, 1977.

Wittrock, M., ed. *The Human Brain.* Englewood Cliffs, N.J.: Prentice-Hall, 1977.

Wooldridge, D. *The Machinery of the Brain.* New York: McGraw-Hill, 1963.

Young, J. *Programs of the Brain.* London: Oxford University Press, 1978.

Index

207